Sense Africa Five Ways

Short safari stories with an expert guide in southern Africa

JENNY BOWEN

WORDCATCHER publishing

SENSE AFRICA FIVE WAYS
Short safari stories with an expert guide in southern Africa

British Library Cataloguing in Publication Data.
A catalogue record for this book is available from the British Library.

Published in the United Kingdom by
Wordcatcher Publishing
www.wordcatcher.com
Facebook.com/WordcatcherPublishing

First Edition: 2017
Paperback ISBN: 9781912056507
Category: Travel Writing

CONTENTS

ACKNOWLEDGEMENTS

I would never have travelled so extensively had my parents not encouraged me to grab life by the horns, so to them I give my grateful thanks for instilling the travel bug. Even from an early age I was challenged to get bread by myself from the local boulangerie at the age of 5, whilst clutching a couple of francs in my small sweaty hand. At the age of 18 I was positively encouraged to travel around the world with my friends, Louise Hardy and Pip Schofield, but I did have to pay for it myself. Mum suggested I cycle to Brittany and back as I was annoying her with my moping around the house when I was not too sure what to do with my life and Dad advised me to take a short-term expedition role in Ecuador rather than a rather more mundane job radio-tracking hares in Buckinghamshire. Thank you for simply letting me do lots of rather exciting stuff with the knowledge that all would be OK at home. However, I have agreed with them that I tell them the crazy stuff that I have done only after the event! Mum, do not worry, I will never, *ever*, do a bungee jump again; four times is enough, promise.

To the person who was the initiator to all things Africa, my thanks go to Jeremy Hill. I'd never have had any of these experiences if it hadn't been for Jeremy.

He was the contact for Raleigh International in Zimbabwe and the reason for my first real job after University. I was applying for the position of ecologist in Zimbabwe and he asked me over the phone "when can you start?" Who does an interview over the phone and then says "yes" whilst having no idea what you are letting yourself into? Well I did and if I had not had that conversation my life might well have taken a completely different course. Jeremy gave me all the scope to get myself into lots of interesting situations and scrapes!

Also, a huge thank you to Karen Paolillo of Turgwe Hippo Trust, in my mind the world's "Hippo Whisperer", who has also written a book and got me thinking that I could do one as well. Karen, you are an inspiration – and a source of a few stories!

My thanks also go to Michael Amphlet, of Quest Overseas, for allowing myself and the now Dr Lucy King free rein to set up Quest Africa. I never really realised how much faith he had in us and it was an incredible opportunity. This was my introduction to the Kingdom of Swaziland as well as Namibia – I mean who gets sent to explore a country for three weeks by themselves?

A huge thank you to Deb MacLeod, Becs Tregarthen and Sam Warren-Mant (the Gorgeous Girls) who have encouraged and supported me and been instrumental in the development of Sense Africa. If my business had not flourished I would never have had half the material to write these anecdotes in the first place. This is for you.

I'd like to thank Sherry Rix, publisher of Travel Africa, who has always been so encouraging when I put a new blog up on my site and for all her positive comments about the stories that I tell. She allowed me to think that someone might even read my book.

Thank you to all of those who are connected to Swaziland; Ted Reilly, Ann Reilly, Mick and Cotz Reilly, Dumi and all the guides and staff of Big Game Parks, Anna McGinn of McGinn Consulting, Elmari Tamen of Tamen Tours, Ernest Masuku and Bongani Dlamini from Swaziland Tourism Authority, Tal Fineburg at Mbuluzi Game Reserve and Kelly White of GEO Tourism.

My thanks also go to Rob Pitt and Ellen McRae who have been rocks of support and encouragement over the years and have never doubted my capabilities.

To Jason Bowen (my brother) and Sam Bowen (my sister in law), thank you. And to my other 'family' members; Tessa Winters, my 'surrogate' Mum, with whom I always had a catering job so I could pay for my next flight into the big wide world, and to Derek, Margaret and Lou Henning who welcomed me as part of their Zimbabwe family.

Thank you to all my other friends who share a similar love of Africa; Jason De Carteret, Keith Leggett, David Cartwright, Margo Bishop, Dawn Wilson and Laura at Travel Wild.

To my dear friends and family who have faith in me; Juliet and Jon Brown, Helen and Nigel Evans, Daphne and Graham Roberts, JY and Julie Rouffiac, and Jenny and Will Watson.

Thank you to David Norrington, my publisher, for being patient with me and giving me a nudge to get things done. All of a sudden, I have three books out in the space of two years; not too shabby for a newbie in the publishing world. Also to Dad and Pip Schofield (The Proof Room) who read the first attempt of this a few years back and gave me some valuable feedback. I am sure it was painful to read. Thank you for your help in the final read through, I hope it was easier to read!

I'd like to thank those who read my blog regularly and comment on it, always good to know that someone is reading my babblings; Phil England, Terry Westcott, John Chapman, Lena Welch, Joy Floyd, Martin How, Gill How, Michela Butler, Phil Smith, Sam Crispin and Glen Nelson.

And thank you to all of you who were surprised and then encouraging when you heard that I was writing a book. Lovely to have such positive reactions.

Finally, I would like to thank genetics. I always loved staying with my Great Aunt Mimi, despite the fact that there was never enough hot water for a decent bath and she spent the whole evening shuttling pans of hot water to and from the bathroom for my brother and myself. I also remember when she called the fire brigade when they were burning the stubble and the hedges had caught alight and the time her dog Titi shed an enormous tick on her bed and we spent ages looking for it. Great Aunt Mimi was an avid traveller and had travelled extensively in China between the wars and helped set up the school in Alice Springs. I have also recently learnt that my great, great aunt Udall travelled throughout Russia many years ago; very pioneering. I guess travel and adventure are firmly ensconced in the female line of my genes, and thank goodness for that.

INTRODUCTION

Many years ago, I was at a networking meeting and a couple of people commented on the stories that I had been regaling them with around the table, and suggested that I should write them up in a book.

Initially, the purpose of the book was to be a great marketing tool for my travel business, Sense Africa. However, with some encouragement, it has now become what you see here today – a series of stories recounting some of my adventures in southern Africa.

As my experience of the wildlife, the landscape, and the people has increased, so too has my love of this part of the world. I began to think about the experiences that I had had in Africa and how I could relate them to the five senses.

I have enjoyed the trip down memory lane in writing this book. The process has made me smile, feel frustrated, be embarrassed, cringe, and laugh. I hope this has the same effect on you and that you can truly sense Africa.

THE LAY OF THE LAND

Africa is the world's second largest and second most-populous continent. At about 30.3 million km², including adjacent islands, it covers 6% of the Earth's total surface area and constitutes 20.4% of its total land area.

I'm always surprised when people refer to 'Africa' as a country, although it is a common occurrence. Africa is made up of 54 countries, all of which are unique and diverse in their own way. It is larger than China, India, the USA, and most of Europe *combined*.

The countries that I explore in this book are all located in southern Africa; Botswana, Mozambique, Namibia, South Africa, Swaziland, and Zimbabwe.

Botswana

Botswana is big game country and its unique and varied ecosystems showcase spectacular untamed wilderness areas forming some of the best wildlife reserves in the world. These include the peace and tranquility of the Okavango Delta, the adrenalin rush of watching prides of lion in Moremi, the wonderful wide open spaces of the Kalahari and the unrivalled elephant herds of Chobe. It is a wildlife watcher's paradise. A visit to Botswana is an absolute treat and the safaris are world-famous for their exclusivity and the likelihood of extraordinary and unique wildlife sightings in secluded locations.

Botswana has a land mass of 581,000 km² and nearly 40% comprises national parks and wildlife reserves, providing large areas for animals to roam. It is a landlocked country, its landscape defined by the Kalahari Desert creating vast arid areas battling with the lush and fertile Okavango Delta that brings life-giving water to the northern part of the country. The Okavango Delta became the 1,000[th] UNESCO (United Nations Educational, Scientific and Cultural Organization) World Heritage site in 2014, and deservedly so. The delta is a myriad of meandering papyrus plant-filled waterways and palm-fringed islands where herds of elephants come to drink. Explore the delta by dugout canoe (mokoro) gently propelled through this magical wonderland by a knowledgeable guide. As the water ripples past and hippos chomp through the undergrowth, allow time to slow down in this serene environment.

Mozambique

Mozambique is known for its pristine coastline, white sandy beaches, and azure blue sea. It boasts excellent water activities like diving, fishing, and swimming, not to mention wonderfully fresh seafood and delicious prawns providing sumptuous meals. There is a vibrant air to Mozambique, incorporating the colourful clothing, funky music, and an exuberance for life that permeates the country. The music is mesmerising and lively and it is easy to become swept up in the passion and buzz of Mozambique. I love Mozambique for its fresh, enticing, and mouth-watering seafood.

Mozambique has a landmass of 801,500 km² and, with an exceptionally long coastline and a myriad of idyllic islands, it is the ultimate getaway for those who want to escape the trappings of tourism and spend time on a private islands or remote beach.

The country is a relatively new tourist destination and as well as sublime islands there are also astounding game parks. These wilderness areas have remained untouched by tourism and the parks still retain an element of inaccessibility. Only the adventurous and those wanting to experience an unspoilt paradise should visit.

Namibia

Namibia is a country of compelling beauty and has a sense of unconfined space and your breath will be taken away by unspoilt landscapes, wide horizons, and clear and unpolluted skies. If you don't like open spaces, this is certainly not the place for you! Rugged, yet fragile, barren, yet beautiful, Namibia is an enchanting wilderness that holds the very essence of Africa.

Whenever I visit Namibia I have an incredible sense of freedom as if I have broken away from the shackles of everyday life.

Namibia has a land mass of 825,000 km² and with a population of just over 2 million has the world's second-lowest population in terms of density, Mongolia topping that list. It is famous for having the oldest desert in the world – the Namib desert – which the country is named after. It holds the highest sand dunes in the world, located at Sossusvlei, one of the world's most ancient plants, *Welwitschia mirabilis*, and boasts the largest population of free-roaming cheetahs.

And there is Etosha National Park, a major sanctuary for a variety of animal species that protects the largest concentration of game in Namibia. It is here that you can go on guided safaris or even on your own self-drives. There's something incredibly special about watching the wildlife come to the floodlit waterholes at night, your own natural theatrical spectacle where you never know what to expect. Simply sit there with a gin and tonic and watch an African wildlife soap opera unfold before your eyes.

South Africa

South Africa, the Rainbow Nation, is so called to highlight the country's cultural diversity, particularly after the wake of apartheid. It is an extraordinary mix of living in harmony with brutal historical events, harsh deserts with rich marine life, dagger like mountains of the Drakensberg with bushveld safari national parks and buzzing metropolises with remote hinterland; it is a colourful and eclectic mix of all that Africa offers. Often it is the beginning of people's love affair with Africa: a visit to Cape Town to climb Table Mountain; to stand at the very end of the continent at the Cape of Good Hope; to listen to the braying of Jackass penguins; to see the whale migration at Hermanus; and to drive the stunning and glorious

Garden Route – a gentle way to be bitten by the Africa bug!

South Africa has around 56 million people and is the 24th most populous nation. It is the 25th largest country with and landmass of is 1,221,000 km². It is one of those iconic countries that everybody has heard of with its incredible highlights of Cape Town and Table Mountain, fantastic wine growing areas (and tasting!) of Stellenbosch, the Garden Route along the south coast, the battle fields of KwaZulu Natal and world famous Kruger National Park where Big Five sightings abound.

Kruger is 19,500 km² in area, and to put it into scale this is about the same size of Wales. It is home to 336 tree species, 49 fish, 34 amphibians, 114 reptiles, 507 birds and 147 mammals, of which the Big Five ar often seen. It is a mecca for wildlife enthusiasts wanting to experience an African wilderness.

If you plan to go to South Africa do not try to see it all, you spend all your time travelling and no time simply enjoying the diversity of culture, scenery and nature.

Swaziland

The Kingdom of Swaziland gives you the opportunity to experience all that southern Africa has to offer in a small and safe environment. Swaziland has varied scenery, from magical mountain ranges to savannah dotted with flat top acacia. It has a host of wildlife parks – some of which you can explore on foot – and it also offers a plethora of exhilarating traditional cultural events. It is heralded as a paradise for lovers of the outdoors. Swaziland is a unique blend of ancient customs woven into everyday life, and for me it is like coming home.

The Kingdom has a population of around 1.2 million and a landmass of 17,300 km² making it the smallest country in Africa. Swaziland is the only country in Africa not practicing multiparty democracy and is one of the world's last remaining absolute monarchies. King Mswati III rules by decree, he also has 15 wives and his father before him, King Sobhuza II, had 70 wives. Imagine all those mothers-in-law! So, if you do visit Swaziland you will probably meet royalty along the way; you just might not realise it.

For such a small kingdom Swaziland packs a punch: it has the world's largest granite monolith, Sibebe Rock; it is home to the largest population of nesting African white-backed vultures in Africa, which are found in Hlane Royal National Park; and it has Ngwenya mine which is the oldest mine in the world dating back 43,000 years. I also think that Swaziland is probably the best white rhino destination in the world and if you do not see white rhino, and have visited both Hlane and Mkhaya reserves, then you have probably been asleep for the duration!

Zimbabwe

Zimbabwe is a magical and mysterious destination that makes you feel compelled to return again and again, as the explorer David Livingstone found out.

The world-famous Victoria Falls are an iconic visitor destination and is one of the seven wonders of the world. The falls stretch 1.7km wide and they plummet 108m. During the wet season the spray from the falls can be seen nearly 50km away; hence the name Mosi-ao-Tunya, or the 'Smoke that Thunders'.

This was the first African country that I visited and it holds special memories for me. Zimbabwe was the instigator of my serious love affair with this beautiful continent.

Zimbabwe has a landmass of 391,000 km² and is renowned for its dramatic scenery. The ancient ruins of Great Zimbabwe are where some of the oldest and largest structures located in southern Africa are found. Unfortunately, it is also known for its political instability, Robert Mugabe at the helm of governing the country and a host of poaching problems within its national parks. Despite this, Zimbabwe has some of the best guides and friendliest people in Africa.

The huge variety of spectacular wilderness areas are an incredible lure to people looking for a true wilderness experience. Explore Mana Pools National Park in a canoe to see one of Africa's largest hippopotamus populations; see elephants galore in Hwange National Park; discover the granite kopjes and historic rock paintings of Matobo Hills; and travel to Gonarezhou National Park for an authentic experience in remote wilderness. It is a truly remarkable country.

SIGHT

Colours in Africa seem to me to appear to be more vibrant, feel warmer, and have greater contrast than anywhere else I know. Sunrise and sunset are the best times, particularly sunset because that's when I'll often have a drink in my hand. It is the burnt orange, golden yellow, and rosy pink that bathes the African bush in the morning and evening that gives me a wonderful sense of well-being.

The sights of Africa are also about simply sitting by a waterhole and watching wildlife coming to drink: whether it be antelope daintily and nervously tiptoeing to the water's edge; the sight of a young elephant gleefully running towards the water with its trunk held aloft in case it trips over it; or a majestic giraffe tentatively and delicately reaching down to the water. Words simply are not enough to describe the sights around a waterhole.

No trip to Africa is complete until I have seen the colourful flitting of bee-eaters, a hippo cavorting in the water, and a kudu antelope watching me with its huge brown eyes like liquid chocolate melting in the heat.

Wild Dogs and an English Girl

I was a greenhorn, blundering around the Zimbabwean bush, learning from my mistakes and enjoying life to the full. I had only been in Africa for two months and I'd already had some memorable experiences, both incredible and scary. I had been charged by a hippo, found a snake in my bathroom, and my car had broken down in the bush leaving me with a 20km walk home. And there was more to come.

I'd heard through the grapevine that there was a pack of wild dogs in *Save Valley Conservancy*, in the south east lowveld of Zimbabwe, which was where I was working. They had recently arrived from Gonarezhou National Park, (also in Zimbabwe), and the park bordered Mozambique. Every day I kept my eyes peeled for these elusive hunters.

The African wild dog, also known as the painted wolf, is an endangered species, and to my mind a sighting of these animals is certainly one to treasure. They are incredible creatures and nearly 80% of all wild dog hunts end with a kill. By comparison, the success rate of lions, (often viewed as the ultimate predator), is only around 30%. I was fascinated by these animals and desperately wanted to see this pack while I was here. Little did I know I was going to get more than I bargained for.

I was driving along one of the many dirt tracks in *Save Valley Conservancy*, when an impala belted across the road in front of me, closely pursued by three wild dogs. The impala didn't stand a chance. I could practically feel the hot breath of the wild dogs on the impala's hind legs. Ten metres off the road the impala met its demise as the wild dogs brought her to the ground. The dogs were already devouring their kill, ripping into her soft underbelly to get to the tasty morsels. As more members of the pack joined the party, the noise of excited and hungry dogs filled the surrounding bush.

The smell of the carcass was assaulting my senses. At first I could smell, and even taste, the iron in the blood of the impala and, in conjunction with a slightly sweet smell, made my nose wrinkle in revulsion. When the wild dogs had ripped open the belly and the innards cascaded out, those smells were mixed with half-digested vegetation, stomach bile, and a putrid stench that made me close my mouth for fear of catching any of the nearby flies that had recently alighted on the carcass. It had only been a couple of minutes since the impala had crossed the road.

At this point, I was about twenty metres away from the kill and the boisterous, chattering dogs, and I tried not to make a noise as I reached for my camera. I had hoped for just a fleeting glimpse of a wild dog. In my wildest dreams, I had never anticipated that I would see a full-blown kill, right in front of me. I watched in fascination.

This was not the end of it. As I drove my vehicle past the kill, the lead dogs took a little bit more interest in the vehicle than I would have liked, and slowly moved towards it. Two dogs broke into a run, chasing after me, I could see them in my wing mirrors. I felt as if I was in the film *Jurassic Park*, where the Tyrannosaurus Rex is getting closer and closer. Those images of the two dogs in my wing mirror will be something I will never forget. The vehicle was now moving at 25km/h, and the dogs were still there. After a terrifying 45 seconds they tired, backing off to a steady trot before turning around to re-join their pack.

It seemed I had been run out of town.

Hungry Hippos

My first time in the African bush was in Zimbabwe. I was staying with my good friend, Karen Paolillo – the person who I was to describe later as the Diane Fossey of hippos. Diane Fossey is an American scientist who undertook an extensive study of mountain gorilla over 18 years and her book *Gorillas in the Mist* was made into the film of the same name starring Sigourney Weaver.

Karen single-handedly saved a pod of hippos during the drought of 1992 in Zimbabwe, as well as countless other animals in the area, and it was during this time that I met her and had my first true bush experience. I stayed with her for five days to learn the basics about the bush so that I would be up to speed when I started my job as ecologist for *Raleigh International*, a UK government-funded youth project.

Karen, and her husband Jean-Roger, were working in *Save Valley Conservancy* and only had a caravan to stay in. Near the caravan, they had erected a small open-sided shelter where they had moved their bed and a small table and chairs. Usually only their cats slept in the caravan, but for the next few nights it was to be my home too.

My first day was a dramatic one. Karen had

identified a pod of hippos that was seriously affected by the drought – they had no water to use during the heat of the day, and food was diminishing rapidly. Hippos need a lot of food to sustain them, mainly bulk, such as grass. They also need water to protect their delicate skin from the fierce sun. Some of the hippos had blisters on their backs and many were on the verge of starvation.

In the morning, we went to feed a young mother who had moved away from the rest of the pod. This involved Karen and me each carrying a large sack of grass and pony nuts. There could have been anything in the bush waiting for us, as well as our hungry hippo. After a good half-an-hour of walking, (with Karen using her in-built compass and me totally relying on the fact that Karen knew where she was going), we arrived at a dry riverbed. Karen told me to wait where I was, not to move, and she left me guarding the food.

I waited, for what seemed like hours. My mind went wild with the thought of being watched by beady eyes, eyeing me up as food, with crazy thoughts that Karen would not come back for me and that I would have to make my own way out of the bush.

My thoughts were interrupted by a large crashing of branches and the sound of a very, very, large hippopotamus coming my way.

Which way to go? I chose neither, stood my ground and waited, whilst holding my breath. Well, it wasn't really a choice to stay there – I was frozen to the spot by fear. Then there was a deathly silence and, some minutes later, Karen appeared. She was impressed that I had stayed where I was, guarding the food. Little did she know that it was due to my inability to take any other action, rather than bravery or sound decision-making.

The crashing had been the mother, charging through the bush to protect her young calf. We left the food on the riverbank at her normal feeding point, and hastily retreated to the relative safety of the bush camp. That was task number one done.

Task number two was to feed the rest of the pod. They were much nearer but more labour-intensive as there were more hungry hippos to feed.

Karen had a wonderful method – the hippos were given a giant sandwich of grass, hay, molasses, and pony nuts. Each hippo would stand next to its neighbour and eat downwards through this sandwich getting all the nutrients and bulk that a famished hippo needs. As Karen knew all the hippos, she knew which were happy eating in a group and which weren't, and where to put the food. It was a well-thought-out process.

I helped with the laying out of each element. We were a bit later than expected so we had to work quickly, and I was told to keep any eye out for greedy ones that might come too early. I could empathise with them as I was getting hungry as well, it had been an exhausting day.

Out of the corner of my eye I sensed a movement, just a slight one, but one that was out of the ordinary. This sense has developed over the years of living in the bush. You have to be on your toes all the time and to expect the unexpected. This has helped me spot elusive wildlife, and get me out of trouble many times. I turned slowly and there was a hippo approaching the sandwich that I was building.

"Er... Karen, there is a hippo here," I said as calmly as I could. Adrenalin was pumping through my body as the hippo swung its head from side to side and then locked its gaze onto us.

"Move slowly backwards and get into the car," Karen said, and we both carefully walked backwards towards her battered old car. I was praying that it would start first time this time, (it was not that reliable). "If it charges... run," She added.

The hippo started moving forwards, picking up speed and with open mouth, built up into a full-blown charge.

"Run!"

We belted for the car, I leapt into it and slammed my door shut although I didn't feel that much safer inside the vehicle. Luckily, the clapped-out car reacted as she should have done, roared into life and Karen reversed it at break-neck speed away from the hippo and the feeding station. The hippo was having none of this and continued to move towards us. Karen couldn't see the hippo as she was looking over her shoulder to steer as she reversed at speed to ensure that we did not hit any trees. I provided her with a helpful commentary of how we were doing.

"Faster, Karen, faster! Its gaining on us! Oh, my God! Faster! Oh, my God!"

The hippo bumped the car's bonnet. It was far too close for comfort. Fortunately, the hippo gave up on the chase and decided that food was a better option. It turned around and lumbered back to its meal, leaving two wide-eyed women in a car with hippo saliva dripping off the bonnet.

Karen looked at me, her face must have been a

mirror of mine – mouth open and eyes bulging – and we burst into a fit of hysterical giggles.

"And that is why hippos can be pretty dangerous," gasped Karen between tears of laughter.

Message received loud and clear!

That night I went to sleep to the melodious sound of honking hippos – what an introduction to life in the bush.

What's in a Name?

Sometimes birds are named for their song. For example, the blacksmith plover sounds like a blacksmith hammering on his anvil – a sharp tink, tink, tink. And the hoopoe is so-called because that's exactly what its call sounds like, a low and sustained 'hoo-poe'.

The African penguin, (yes there are penguins in Africa!), has a donkey-like braying call, and when a whole colony of penguins become vocal your ears certainly know about it. It's commonly known as the jackass penguin, and rightly so.

Some names do not do the species justice. For instance, the African wattled lapwing has smaller wattles (flaps of skin hanging from a bird's chin that are often an enticement for courting) than the white crowned lapwing, which often causes confusion when identifying them at a waterhole.

Why does the African pitta sound a rather dull and boring bird when, in my opinion, it is one of the most colourful birds in Africa? Everyone has the African pitta on their ultimate bird spotting list. It has a white and black stripy head with olive green back, pink chin, red undercarriage, and luminous blue wing-spots visible when it flies. Basically, it's a flying rainbow.

As for the broad-billed roller, don't get me started. It has extraordinary lilac/purple underparts, but you wouldn't know it from its name. Its bill is not that broad, but its lilac chest and lower parts are something to sing about...

Then there are exotically-named birds such as the African paradise fly catcher, the gorgeous bush shrike (which really is gorgeous), and the greater double-collared sunbird. Now, they *are* named correctly. I think that after a while the person naming birds got a little bit bored and resorted to naming them after their more obvious characteristics; the red winged starling has red wings (although I would call them russet), the yellow-billed stork is a stork with a yellow bill, and the long-tailed paradise whydah does in fact have a very, very long tail. So long, I wonder how it manages to leave the ground, let alone fly.

There are also some wonderfully-named birds where you would have had to smoke something illegal to come up with their names. For example, the secretary bird has some plumes sticking out of the top of its head that may or may not resemble 18th century clerks with pens tucked into their wigs.

And the green, red-throated and pink-throated twinspot has two white spots on every small feather, but you would have to hold one to find this out.

Quite often, birds are named after how they look, so once you have tracked down your singing bird, you may be able to take a guess at its name. Once you have heard your bird and identified it, there is a host of interesting information that surrounds each species – admittedly some more interesting than others. Ask your guide about local beliefs surrounding the birds that you see; you may be surprised by the similar or wildy different folklore that is attached in different areas.

The hamerkop is just one such bird with a story to tell. It has a slightly curved beak and a distinctive crest at the back of its head that resembles a hammer, hence its name; another creative name for another plain, brown bird of Africa. Remarkably, this average-sized brown bird has numerous myths, legends, and local beliefs surrounding it. It seems to have taken far more than its fair share of mythical stories and sayings, making it rather an interesting sighting in the bush. However, most of the tales seem to be about death or contracting some hideous disease, depending on the culture you listen to.

The first legend that I heard about the hamerkop was that if you ever looked into water at the same time as one, it would be the harbinger of death. I wasn't sure whose death it would be, but it makes me think twice about looking at any water with a hamerkop in the vicinity. Other legends say that if one flies over your house someone close to you has recently died. It is also believed by the Malagasy of Magadascar that if you disturb a hamerkop's nest you will develop leprosy. The Kalahari bushmen believe that if you rob eggs from a hamerkop's nest you will be struck by lightning. All of which, to my mind, is a bit of doom and gloom and makes this a bird you'd not want to mess with. Would you risk disturbing a hamerkop's nest, at the tiny possibility of contracting leprosy?

Trapped by Wildlife

It was a typical morning in Africa with Karen. We had risen with the sun, been down to check the hippos that Karen was studying, and were back at the house by breakfast time. I call her place a 'house'; in fact Hippo Haven is more than a house – it is a beautiful thatched home on the side of the River Turgwe in Zimbabwe, built and sculpted by herself and her husband, Jean-Roger. There are no glass windows, just frames of mosquito netting, so the house is cool in the heat of the day and filled with light.

Karen and Jean-Roger have a lot of cats, and they are kept inside most of the time to protect them from the wildlife. Domestic cats are high up on the snack list, and they also don't have much bush sense, being a bit soft around the ears when it comes to surviving in the wild. This is in contrast to their distant cousins, servals, genets, wild cats, and caracals.

The particular morning in question, I was sitting inside with the sun streaming into the sitting room, surrounded by cats and contentedly reading my book. The cats were animated and attentively looking out through the mesh of the front door and playing games with each other, hissing, swiping, and cavorting along the window ledges. Karen was out the back checking on the reservoir for the house and Jean-Roger had gone in the truck to check on snares in the area.

Arthur, a large warthog with ginormous tusks, had come for his regular morning visit and breakfast and was munching on pony nuts outside the back door. Karen often fed wildlife that came to Hippo Haven, and Arthur had a special place in her heart. He always came to the back door and was fed on a regular basis: the back-door area was his and his alone. Only Karen was allowed into Arthur's area and anyone else, including Jean-Roger, was charged at, and that is a pretty scary experience. Arthur is the size of a fat labrador and he's made purely from muscle, sinew, bone, and guts. A large warthog could break your shins if it decided to charge at you, and Arthur was certainly a charger!

I had tried to exit out of the back door when Arthur was there before, but playing chicken with a warthog that large is not something I would advise. As soon as I had opened the door he was alert, tail up, watching me with his beady eyes. He made a short mock charge towards me and that was enough to send me scurrying back inside. The damage he could have done to me could have been painful and that was not even taking into account the size of his tusks. His tusks alone could have disembowelled me. I had enormous respect for Arthur, I would always let him be.

Living where they do, Karen and Jean-Roger have a bathroom in their house, but without a toilet. The toilet was of the long drop variety (a big deep hole, and the name comes from how long it takes for your 'business' to drop). Ultimately, a 'long drop' becomes a 'short drop' as it fills up. The long drop was left behind as a legacy from when they had camped in the bush and before they had built their wonderful house. They did not want to build a septic tank as it was near to the river and with just the two of them living there it wasn't considered a necessity. So, the toilet was not part of the house. It was an outhouse. And it was at this point that I needed to go to the loo.

As I opened the front door and turned right towards the long drop, my sixth sense kicked in. I glanced over my shoulder to my left, and there, only 2m away from me, was an unhappy cobra. It was standing up at around chest height, its hood was out and it was not pleased to see me.

I took all this information in at record speed and my brain engaged into retreat mode. I must have looked like Scooby Doo as I reversed in mid-air, whilst doing those circular motions with my legs, and slammed the door shut, making sure that all the cats were safe inside.

"Karen, there is a large snake outside the front door, and it's not happy," I yelled.

I peered out of the front door and the cobra was still there, still looking hacked off with life. It was standing about 70cm high, its hood was fully extended making it look even more threatening than it had done moments before and it was undulating gently as if swaying in a breeze, although, there was no wind. It was as thick as a large salami and had characteristic black and pale yellow stripes across its body. It was a Mozambique spitting cobra.

Mozambique spitting cobras are large, robust snakes that average in length at about 1.2m as adults, but can grow to 1.6m long. It spits from any position, raised or on the ground, can eject venom up to 2.4m, and often goes for the eyes. Untreated, its venom can cause blindness, so it is a pretty formidable snake. It is considered the most dangerous snake after the mamba.

These cobras sport a chocolate-brown or grey-brown colour on top, with a salmon-pink or orange underbelly. The throat has a couple of irregular, broad bands across it that are clearly visible if the snake were to face you with its hood spread.

I find snakes fascinating. I have seen a python in the process of digesting a small antelope, (it had serious stomach ache as the horns stuck out through its skin). I've had black mambas slither across the path in front of me, seen boomslangs magnificently coiled in trees, and encountered cobras with their hoods out. All are memorable, if not heart-in-the-mouth experiences. I was never in any danger, and these snakes just carried on with their own business. Having said that, it is certainly advisable to have somebody with you who knows what they're talking about. If you are lucky, or unlucky, (however you look at it), to see a snake while accompanied by a guide, you will also learn an awful lot about that species, as sightings are rare, and you will also be in safe hands. Having someone knowledgeable on hand makes all the difference on safari.

Snakes are secretive animals and they 'hear' an approaching animal by sensing the vibrations on the ground. More often than not they will slither away into nearby vegetation as they are more afraid of you than you need to be of them. They have an amazing ability to blend into the surrounding area, so even if you are trying to look for them it can prove difficult. And snakes will not attack a human being unless they are provoked, so do not go and poke a snake with a stick, or you'll be asking for trouble!

This snake was agitated, the extended hood was a big clue, and I could see those distinctive bands on its neck as it stood erect above the ground. Definitely a Mozambique spitting cobra and a large one too.

Unfortunately, the cats were not helping the situation by hissing through the netting and agitating the snake into an even worse mood than it was already in. I struggled to keep the cats away from the mesh windows as maybe the cobra could spit its venom through the netting? Who knows? I was not ready to find out.

It was then that I realised my dilemma, I needed the toilet but I could not go out of the front door for fear of meeting the cobra and I could not leave the house by the back door because of Arthur. I weighed up the options of blindness versus broken shins, and came to the conclusion that neither was attractive. I could not hold on for long, and, from past experience, the wildlife was probably going to be around for a while. So, I chose option three.

"Karen!" I yelled, "I'm going to pee in your bath!"

The Stuff of Nightmares

When I first lived in Zimbabwe, I was given an old farmhouse that the first Europeans had built back in the times when there were vast herds of game wandering across the plains of Africa. It was a beautiful, five-bedroom house, built out of teak, but it hadn't been lived in for ages. I was not too concerned by this, as it had four walls and provided a roof over my head. With the house came an enormous, overrun garden, a large kitchen with a wood burner, the use of the swimming pool in the compound, and a large game fence to protect us from the wildlife.

What I had not banked on was the wildlife *inside* the compound. As I moved into my new house, Derek, the landowner, asked me how I was with snakes. I was not too sure whether this was a trick question. I mean, I have not handled that many snakes but they do not give me the heebie-jeebies, if that was what Derek was asking. He promptly gave me a shotgun and told me to keep it under my bed – Mozambique spitting cobras had a penchant for this house and I was advised to shoot from the hip. I was told that if I shot from the shoulder I would probably dislocate it. I was left holding the shotgun with my mouth wide open. I did not sleep well that night, even with a loaded gun under the bed. No wonder the house was empty... or was it?

As well as the house I also lived in a small, round, mud hut with my own little vegetable patch. I spent many a night there by myself, which at times was rather disconcerting as there was no door, and I had heard a leopard 'coughing' nearby one night. Most of the time, however, I was project managing a group of volunteers who were helping me with my scientific survey work. When they arrived, the area changed and became a sea of tents – living quarters, medical facilities, and cooking areas. And it was outside one of these tents that a mini adventure began.

Late one night I was walking over to the medical tent when I noticed four big, fat, hairy legs poking out of a hole in the ground, right in front of the entrance to the tent. This was going to be trouble.

The next morning, I called Epheus over to get his opinion on the matter. Epheus was my camp guard, a wizened, elderly, local guy who had worked in the area for Lord knows how many years, and was an oracle on all things in the African bush.

"Aah, it eez not gud Meees Janny," said Epheus, while shaking his head. "This eez very bad," he continued, peering into the hole.

"I know that," I said, frustrated, "but can you do anything about it?" As an afterthought I added, "And you mustn't kill it!" My ecological background was kicking in, and wanted to save every single living creature.

Epheus smiled, shook his head in exasperation and walked away, leaving me dumbfounded. He had got used to my philosophy about not killing things, although I am sure that he did not believe in it himself. He returned with a pickaxe and a blade of grass - not the usual implements for removing a big fat hairy spider. But he was the expert after all, so I watched with curiosity. By now there were a growing number of people peering into the hole and shivering at the thought of a rather large spider just outside the medical tent. Ironic, as this species, the baboon spider, had a nasty and poisonous bite, so if you were to be anywhere when that happened, this would be the place for it.

Epheus looked at me with a knowing smile, and delicately put the blade of grass into the hole and jiggled it around with his left hand. Meanwhile his right hand was raised above his head, brandishing the pickaxe. His left hand was still working hard with the blade of grass and then, suddenly, he froze, and we collectively held our breath. The pickaxe came down with full force and he started digging up a considerable area before throwing the pick axe away and surveying his destruction.

Out of nowhere loomed the spider, boulders cascading off its back and probably not too happy with its current situation. Epheus pounced on the spider, laying his right hand flat across the thorax of this monstrosity, and then manoeuvring his fingers around so he could pick it up without getting bitten. The spider was nearly as big as his hand with its legs outstretched and, as Epheus brought it close to my face, I could see its poisonous, biting, mouth parts clearly. Too close for my liking, far too close. But I did not flinch.

This was evidently not the reaction that Epheus had wanted from me, so he turned and did the same to Lucy, the medic for the resident group. She shrieked, thus providing the desired effect. Epheus proceeded to chase Lucy. A wizened old man waving a big fat hairy spider and all the while cackling with laughter, hobbling after a very scared lady. I was just glad that it wasn't me.

I often get asked about snakes, spiders, and other creepy crawlies, they are in the top ten of people's phobias and are the last thing that many visitors want to see. Admittedly, Africa has got its fair share of these creatures and some of them are of gargantuan proportions – such as our baboon spider. However, if you take the right precautions, it is unlikely that you will have a run-in with these pesky critters, unless you actively choose to do so.

After my spider incident, I seemed to attract all things deadly. The next time I was at a different campsite. It was dusk, and I had a wonderful camp fire going. The fact that the fire was brilliant was partly my downfall because it attracted certain species of creepy crawlies to it.

I was working in the *Bubiana Conservancy*, Zimbabwe, providing scientific survey work to look at the grass biomass across the whole of the conservation area. This would help in managing land use in the future. I had a team of volunteers with me, whom I'd trained to do the analysis, and they were walking numerous transects (straight routes) day in, day out, and then returning to the camp.

We were all sitting around the fire on upturned buckets that we were going to use the following day to create pitfall traps. There was movement in the twilight and a not-so-small and undesirable creature with lots of legs darted into the flickering light of the campfire. It was a Transvaal thick-tailed scorpion, *Parabuthus transvalicus.* This variety of scorpion is one of the few that has a sting that is capable of killing an adult human and, although I was vaguely aware of this, I was still naïve and I hadn't fully got the full picture about this deadly little critter.

I thought the sensible thing to do would be to cover it with one of the upturned buckets, leave it there for the night, and then release it in the morning. I didn't think there was any point in trying to return it to the bush because it would just be attracted by the firelight again, and I would probably end up spending the whole night walking backwards and forwards with a scorpion in a bucket.

I carefully covered the scorpion with my bucket and went to fetch a new bucket to sit on. We all carried on chatting, until our conversation was interrupted by another guest – another scorpion was in our midst. Again, I carefully placed my bucket over the scorpion and got myself another one to sit on. This happened many times throughout the night, and I began seriously to question my choice of campsite. It seemed as if I had created a settlement in the middle of a *Parabuthus transvalicus* convention.

Eventually, we decided it was time to turn in and I left the camp fire area with the buckets dotted around the area, all thirteen of them. I was amazed there were so many, and I was rather concerned about the safety of the camp site, with risk assessments reeling through my mind. There seemed, to my mind, to be an inordinate number of scorpions knocking around.

I had a rather restless night's sleep, and in the morning I got up early as I didn't want the scorpions to bake in the sun in their personalised prisons. I gingerly removed the first bucket to find no scorpion underneath. This was the same for the second, the third, the fourth, indeed for all thirteen buckets.

I was perplexed and confused. Where had they all gone? How could they have got out?

It was only later, when I looked up *Parabuthus transvalicus* in my identification book to learn more about this creepy crawly, that I found it was locally called the thick-tailed *burrowing* scorpion. I then realised that I had spent the whole night covering the *same* scorpion, and each time it had burrowed its way out of its prison, carried on its merry way only to be captured again! Rather embarrassing from a scientific perspective!

If you want to avoid snakes, spiders, and creepy crawlies then I would advise travel during the African winter months. They don't like being out in the cold, and believe me Africa can get very cold at night. In the southern hemisphere this is June, July, and August. It is too cold for snakes to be particularly active, spiders prefer to take refuge from the lower temperatures, no self-respecting mosquito will be out, and other insects and creepy crawlies are rarely seen.

There is always something unexpected to see on safari, whether it be fat or thin, hairy or scaly, humongous or teeny – Africa has it all. Even if you don't particularly like these critters, give them a bit of respect, as they can be surprising... and certainly fascinating.

The Bone Thrower

Immersing yourself in African cultures can truly enhance your travel experience. There will always be something to remember about your visit to Africa: whether it is simply conversing with your local guide and learning about his or her lifestyle; or taking time to visit a school for the morning and exchanging knowledge and views; or spending a few days in a local community to truly get an understanding of how they interact. There is always something to learn.

I encourage visitors to engage as much as possible with the local people whilst they are on their safari. Initially, guests think that they have more to offer, but after a few hours it is abundantly clear that the flow of information is both ways and it can often be a humbling experience for overseas visitors.

Across the continent, Africans have a lovely tradition of offering guests food and drink as soon as they enter their homestead, even when, at times, they have so little. And you will always see older relations being looked after within the homestead. Their wisdom and knowledge have been passed down to the younger generations. Once you get speaking to local people, you realise they have the same wants and needs and hopes and aspirations that we have: the desire for their children to be educated; to have somewhere safe to live; to go to university; to have a mobile phone; to be with someone they love; to travel; the list is endless.

Staying in a local community is often the highlight of a holiday, although this is probably not most people's idea of why they are travelling before they leave home.

While staying in Swaziland I encourage people to visit Shewula, a community in the north-east of Swaziland on the Lubombo plateau with stunning views over the *Lubombo Conservancy*. The community is made up of around 80,000 people, most of whom get by on a subsistence-style of living and they rely on other family members to bring in a small income. The community took it upon themselves to create *Shewula Mountain Camp*, a rustic-style lodge made up of eight rondavels (traditional round huts) set on the outskirts of the village. It is run by the locals for the benefit of AIDS orphans and other vulnerable children in the community.

There are several things that you can do while you stay there, and the local guides are fantastic. You can be guided around the local homesteads, learn about their traditional way of life, visit the local schools, go to a church service, or eat the local cuisine. There is so much to see it can be exhausting for your eyes!

One of the most memorable sights I've had there was when I visited the local Sangoma, or traditional healer. Visitors often confuse a traditional healer with a witch doctor. A traditional healer gives positive advice and medication for those that need it, whereas witch doctors are reputed to cast evil over individuals.

In all my time in Swaziland I have never knowingly met a witch doctor, but I have met plenty of healers. The first time I saw one I was with a group of students from the UK and had arranged to meet the local traditional healer, Jeluga. I knew Jeluga personally as I had been working closely with him. We drove to Jeluga's homestead and waited until we were summoned to see him. Before entering his hut, I took my shoes off, clapped three times and put a coin on the ground. Everyone is traditionally asked to do this, even the locals. I then entered the gloomy rondavel welcoming the coolness of the mud hut. We all sat down in front of Jeluga. Nobody said a word – we were rather in awe of the apparition that sat before us.

Jeluga was sitting in his finery of traditional dress, sporting an incredible headgear of feathers and beads, and holding a sort of fly swatter made of a zebra tail. Once I had grown accustomed to the dimly-lit interior I began to take in my surroundings: jars of leaves and coloured concoctions littered the floor; a few skulls of unidentifiable animals were nailed to the walls; bunches of leaves and twigs hung suspended from the ceiling; and an enormous python skin circumnavigated the hut. It was an Aladdin's cave of treasures.

Jeluga greeted us seriously, and we all smiled

nervously and fidgeted as we sat down on the grass mats. He took some snuff, snorted it, coughed and spluttered, and then started to shake a small purse which rattled ominously. We were going to have the bones thrown for us.

It is a privilege to be invited into a traditional healer's house. They are revered in Swaziland and 80% of the population will consult a traditional healer as they are considered to be physicians, herbalists, prophets, priests, and diviners all rolled into one. Therefore, they have a great deal of responsibility and status within the community. Most locals will choose to pay for a traditional healer before consulting a doctor. As a result, traditional healers are often busy people and I was grateful that Jeluga had set time aside for our visit.

The bones were thrown on the mat and we all leaned forward in anticipation – not that we could 'read' the bones, but curiosity had overpowered us. There, on the mat, were two dice, two dominoes, an assortment of vertebrae with differently-coloured wire around them, cowrie shells, toe bones complete with claws, coins, glass beads, feathers, and more bones of indeterminate origin or function.

Jeluga moved some of the bones and other objects around, studied them, and communed with his dead relatives for advice. Healers can converse with their ancestors and their ancestors can converse with anybody else's ancestors that are in the room. In essence there was a lot of chatting going on of which we were unaware.

After what seemed an age, Jeluga asked us

whether we had any questions, questions that were applicable to the whole group rather than to an individual. The obvious question was how the expedition was going to progress, and luckily the answer was that it was all going to go well and we would have a positive outcome. Traditional healers are only allowed to relay positive news. It is against their principles to give out bad news.

Then came a flood of questions such as, "What do you use the Python skin for?", "What is in this pickle jar, and what is it used for?", and "Why have you got a broken record in your thatch roof?" All perfectly reasonable questions responded to with rather obscure answers.

It was fascinating listening to Jeluga explain how his ancestors had directed him to a specific bone or guided him to a unique rock or led him to a unique plant. I admit though that I took it all with a pinch of salt. I mean, really, could he genuinely talk to his ancestors? And could his ancestors actually talk to my ancestors? To my mind it was a little far-fetched.

After we had left the session, James, one of the students, decided that he would like to have a personal reading with Jeluga and, of course, it was easily arranged. James entered the hut and was in there for about fifteen minutes. He came out looking bewildered and a little pale. Jeluga motioned me over.

"He should call home and speak with his sister," he told me, "She is fine now, but she has had serious chest pains and she would like to speak to her brother. Jenny, please make sure he calls her."

I promised that I would do so, and went over to

speak to James. He had told the group that the bones had been thrown for him and Jeluga had immediately asked about his sister, saying that he could see that they were really close. Jeluga had said that she was in a bit of pain but everything was good now, however she would like to hear from him. James does, in fact, have a twin sister, and I'm positive that there was no way that Jeluga would have known this.

I did offer my mobile but James said that he would make the call a couple of days later when we next had access to a landline. I didn't think any more of it and put the whole incident to the back of my mind.

Three days later, James came over to me looking decidedly ill and gaping a bit like a goldfish.

"You are never going to believe this," he said. "I've just called home and spoken to my sister. She was really pleased to talk with me and said she had been thinking of me. Recently she had been in a car accident and, on impact with another car, the airbag on the driver's side had failed to deploy, so she'd hit the steering wheel. She has a fractured sternum."

This revelation did not take long to filter through my brain. "Oh, my God," I said, slightly amazed, "Jeluga was right." And then I said, "How could he have known?" We were both stunned.

James went to tell the rest of the group his news and to let them make their own decision about what had just happened. Maybe Jeluga can speak to his ancestors. Who knows?

Whatever the outcome, seeing a traditional healer at work is truly memorable, if a bit unnerving.

Relocating Elephants

When I was first in Zimbabwe, I worked in *Save Valley Conservancy*, situated in the south-east Lowveld. It was in 1992, and the rains had not yet come, people were starving, and animals were dying. This was not the best first impression of Africa. The earth was sun-baked to such an extreme that waterholes had become dust bowls, river crossings were no longer needed as you could drive anywhere, and the nearby swimming pool was waterless as the local wildlife had drunk it dry with the help of evaporation.

Where I was based was not the worst hit – further south in Gonerezhou National Park the game there were suffering horrifically. Gonerezhou was famous for teeming wildlife, in particular the massive herds of elephants that inhabit the area. It is a beautiful part of the country and exceptionally wild in some places, truly the essence of Africa. In 1992 it was more accurately described as an elephant graveyard. Gonerezhou was littered with the skulls of elephants, it was a place of death, and the stench was indescribable.

Action needed to be taken, and elephants saved. So, the members of *Save Valley Conservancy* came up with a plan for relocating some of the elephants out of Gonerezhou and into the conservancy area. In *Save* there were alternative sources of water and the game was being fed to keep them alive. If just some of the elephants could be saved in the same manner then it was worth a try.

One early morning, there was a group of us waiting in the bush for the arrival of the largest elephant ever to be relocated in Zimbabwe. We had heard that an enormous bull had been captured, put into a crate, loaded onto a truck, and was being driven up to *Save*. An incredible feat as, at the time, it was the largest animal ever to be moved in Zimbabwe, and could potentially herald the beginning of a mass move of elephants and other game out of drought-stricken areas. We were rather anxious as to how the elephant would react to its journey and to its new surroundings.

It is generally advisable to put a newly-moved animal into a boma (holding pen) for a while to allow it to get used to its new surroundings and become acclimatised to the different sounds and smells. However, with such a large animal, this was not going to be feasible, so the plan was to open the crate and allow the elephant to walk out into a remote part of the conservancy area where there were fewer distractions and the vegetation was similar to that in its previous home. So, there we all were, waiting for the newest addition to *Save*.

He arrived mid-morning and the crate was positioned so that the gate pointed towards the bush. There were several trucks and cars parked a respectable distance away and we all waited with bated breath. The door was opened... and nothing happened. He just stood there, watching, waiting, for what I do not know. He was not coming out, that was clear. Half an hour passed and nothing happened. A few people left, but I still watched with anticipation to see the first elephant released into *Save Valley Conservancy*. Still, he did not budge.

Then, with no warning at all, there was a trumpet

and four tonnes of African elephant charged out of the crate, scattering complacent viewers aside and leaving a wake of destruction in the form of broken trees and a dented truck. And then there was silence. That was it. One elephant introduced into *Save Valley Conservancy*. Rather an anti-climax.

That is the excitement of being in the African bush – in the blink of an eye it had all happened and there was now a huge bull elephant rampaging around my stomping ground. I would have to be a bit warier when out in the bush around here from now on. And that made life a bit more exciting in the following months as our paths crossed on a number of occasions.

He was the first of many elephants to be introduced, some of which went well and others that did not. One resulted in the demise of a newly-introduced elephant. The decision to put an animal out of its misery is a difficult one to take, especially if it is an elephant. It is something that I will never forget, and a decision that will always stay with me. This is not a happy subject, but Africa is full of life and death and you see it every day. It is really raw and it makes you appreciate life to the full.

I had been tasked with building several bomas for younger, and therefore smaller, relocated elephants to stay in so that they could get used to their surroundings. On release, we hoped that they would stay in the vicinity and not head back to their previous home. The drought had seriously affected wildlife throughout most of southern Africa, and people were doing anything to save as many animals as possible.

We had thirteen elephants in the bomas and they

had been there for a week. They were all youngsters and each had endured the traumatic 12-hour journey in a number of hot and confined containers. On arrival, they had been dehydrated. Despite this, most of the elephants seemed to be bouncing back but there was one who was not doing so well. He had chronic diarrhoea and we had done everything in our means to help him but he was getting weaker by the day.

Graham, the manager of the reserve, came to see me in the morning of that fateful day.

"Jenny, I need your advice," he said.

I clambered into the Land Rover and we drove the short distance to the boma. The sight that I beheld was a sad one and it is forever engraved in my mind. The elephant was lying on its left side and there were flies buzzing around his eyes and inside his mouth, he hadn't even got the energy to brush away these critters. Graham and I climbed the walls of the boma and respectfully approached this magnificent animal. It was heart-wrenching to see this marvellous animal lying helpless in the dirt, pitiful and lacklustre.

"Graham, you have got to shoot it. You have got to put it out of its misery," I said.

"I know, I just wanted somebody else to say it."

And so it was that I had put the nail in the coffin for this animal. I waited with the elephant whilst Graham went into his house to get his rifle. The elephant rumbled a little bit and closed his eyes every now and again, this was the only movement that he made. I didn't want to leave him alone.

Ten minutes later Graham climbed back into the boma and we both stood next to each other and with a knowing nod he placed the rifle near to the elephant's head. We, as human beings, always like to anthropomorphise, but I truly believe that the elephant knew what was going to happen, as he gave a massive sigh and closed his eyes with finality, never to open them again.

The crack of the bullet made me jump and the elephant went into spasms and then lay there, motionless.

I didn't dare look at Graham as we both silently climbed out of the boma to walk towards his house. We went straight into his office and he opened the fridge and handed me a beer. It was 10.30 in the morning. We finished the beer, having not uttered a word, and started a second one.

Graham then turned to me and said in a whisper, "I never want to have to do that ever again." he said in a whisper.

"And I never ever want to see that again," I said choking back a few tears.

Africa does that to you, it lifts you up and then dumps you in the dirt. It is an emotional roller coaster of a ride, but I would never exchange it.

Traditional Dancing in Swaziland

"Where is your sarong?" asked the driver of the combi, accusingly.

I sat smugly in the back of the taxi van knowing that I was suitably and respectfully dressed for this traditional occasion. The lady tourist, to whom the driver was talking, mumbled that she didn't know she had to wear a sarong. She asked anxiously whether she would be allowed into the Reed Dance. The answer was an emphatic 'No', along with the murmurings of disapproval from the locals in the minivan. She was wearing shorts.

All over Swaziland, whether it be a small traditional homestead or one of the Kingdom's largest traditional ceremonies, ladies are not allowed to wear shorts. By far the most acceptable attire is a traditional sarong with either the Swazi flag or one with King Mswati III on it. Even if this is wrapped around your shorts it is acceptable.

Traditionally, girls wore only a string of beads until they were eight years old and then they would add a short skirt, and at the age of 15, a long skirt. However, at the Reed Dance, maidens wear large tasselled belts around their midriff (and not much else) and also bare their breasts to the world. I could understand the confusion of the hapless tourist in the combi, her knees were probably the least private part of her body showing from her perspective.

I leaned toward the driver. "But there are sarongs on sale just outside the gates of the palace aren't there?" I queried. "Surely she could buy one there?" There was a murmur of discussion in the taxi and the group consensus was that this would probably be the case.

"It should cost about E50," I told the lady, which was about £3. She smiled gratefully. I remembered only too well what it was like to be a stranger at such events.

We drove along a dirt road, avoiding goats, cattle, feral dogs, and a host of people making their way towards Ludzidzini – the royal residence in Lobamba.

Swaziland had suddenly become a hive of colourful activity: it was the end of the annual eight-day Umhlanga Reed Dance festival.

Over the first four days of the festival, maidens gathered in groups to cut and collect tall reeds from all over Swaziland, and sometimes in Mozambique, bind them, and return to Ludzidzini. During these days, I had seen hundreds of maidens standing in the back of cattle and army lorries, singing and dancing as they went to cut the reeds for the Queen Mother, Ndlovukazi. The atmosphere was one of unity and jubilation and quite often traffic was halted, as these maidens had priority over absolutely everything. A few days previously I had seen a whole market stop trading to watch and cheer the maidens as they walked by, proudly carrying their reeds aloft in the sunshine.

After four days of work, the fifth is one of rest and preparation for one of Africa's largest and most colourful cultural spectacles. Maidens wash in the rivers, plait their hair, and sing in the streets. There is a fabulous party feel with an air of expectation of something special on the horizon.

On the second Monday of the celebrations, tens of thousands of maidens gather at Ludzidzini Royal Residence for the final day of celebration of the ancient Umhlanga custom. Girls have travelled from villages all over the tiny nation to congregate and perform in front of, and pay homage to, the Swazi Queen Mother. The girls present their cut reeds in bundles to the Queen Mother, and the protective *Guma* (reed fence) around her homestead will be rebuilt using them.

I climbed out of the combi, directed the lady tourist towards a delighted sarong seller, and joined the throng of people flowing through the gates of Ludzidzini. I continued to follow the visitors up the hill towards the main part of the palace. There were a few police here, checking that visitors were adhering to the rules of attire and behaving in an orderly manner. It was a beautifully serene experience.

I don't know what I was expecting, but I couldn't believe how many girls were there – thousands of them, all dressed in traditional Swazi attire of vibrantly-coloured sashes, skirts, and jewellery. All were bare-footed, bare-breasted, smiling, and forming an orderly queue. Each of them held their own bundle of reeds. It was an extraordinary spectacle.

Female police officers were keeping order and they directed groups of about 50 similarly-dressed girls, all dancing in unison and singing their hearts out, into the Queen's Kraal (homestead) to lay their reeds. This was a private part of the ceremony and visitors were not allowed to watch the actual laying of the reeds, only the entering and leaving.

The policewomen really were the Fashion Police. They checked every girl to make sure she was wearing the correct traditional clothing, and in the correct way. Woe betide any girl who was not showing her breasts properly or her skirt was too long!

After laying their reeds, the girls snaked out of the Queen's Kraal and into a massive stadium, where everyone could see them in their full glory. I made my way to the stadium and found a seat near the VIP area. It was an incredible view. More and more girls poured into the arena, until there were around 60,000. Well, that was my guess, however many people there were it was mind boggling. The newspapers on the following day said that there were 70,000 girls. What a sight!

An enormous procession of girls, in a most organised and respectful manner, flowed past the grandstand, rocking in a vocal celebration of maiden's chastity and purity. Different groups had a slightly different take on the same dance and sang a slightly different song, all holding their machetes and shields and dancing in wonderful synchronisation. This was directed by a leader blowing a whistle to keep them all in rhythm.

There didn't seem to be that many people watching the event, probably about a thousand. In comparison to the number performing we were a small part of the event. It was weird to see so many more people performing than spectating.

In front of me was a family obviously waiting to see their daughter go past. They had a massive picnic of pap (the local staple food that looks like semolina), roast chicken, and tomatoes, and were digging into it whilst having a hilarious conversation about something. I didn't know what they were talking about as it was in siSwati, the local language, but it still made me smile as they all fell about laughing in an animated way. Watching them laugh became infectious and I found myself smiling with them and before long I was laughing with them too.

Then they saw their daughter. Mum stood up, waved exuberantly and shouted at her daughter, "Nomsa, up here," or something to that effect, and the surrounding crowd all laughed with her.

Most teenagers back in the UK would have been acutely embarrassed by this outward display of recognition and affection. Instead of trying to ignore her mother and pretend that it was some mad woman, 'Nomsa' stopped dancing with her cohort, turned to the crowd, spotted Mum, (who was still waving a chicken leg and squealing with delight), waved back with double the enthusiasm and with pride all over her face.

The whole family then got up and waved, along with the crowd around them, so I thought I might as well join in and wave to Nomsa as well. The grin we all received was blinding. What a privilege to be part of this extraordinary spectacle, to be accepted by all the people around me and to be waved at by a stranger in the middle of a public performance.

It didn't stop with Nomsa, other girls got a similar reception from family members and the crowd in the vicinity. Obviously, I joined in whenever I could!

The delightful thing about this event is that it is not publicised, it is undertaken by the maidens for the Queen Mother, for their families, and for themselves. The timing of the event is never released until a month or so before, so planning to see it can be pot luck. The dates are set around the full moon and the event is held towards the end of August or the beginning of September.

The Reed Dance is a visual celebration of the girls' camaraderie, solidarity, and chastity. Once seen, never forgotten.

Water Safaris

Seeing wildlife from the water gives a completely different perspective, and is also a more chilled-out experience and definitely less dusty!

Two million years ago the Cubango River flowed from Angola into Botswana, where it became the Okavango River and formed a large inland sea called Lake Makgadikgadi. The area to this day is exceptionally flat and, with a small gradient of only 60m over a distance of 450km, the water slowly fans out over a vast area creating a unique system of waterways with very little energy to flow anywhere.

The Okavango Delta – *The river that never finds the sea* – is one of the world's largest inland deltas. It is a peaceful and isolated haven set in Botswana's harsh Kalahari Desert. It is often described as the jewel of the Kalahari as it sustains at least 9,000 species of flora and fauna, many of which are endemic or rare. This unique ecosystem of 15,000 km^2 is a seasonal wetland oasis.

I was staying in the heart of the Okavango and one of the best ways to explore the area is on a mokoro safari. This is a traditional way to experience the delta. A mokoro (plural is mekoro) is a wooden dugout canoe. Local communities have used the mokoro as a reliable form of transport for centuries; for fishing, collecting firewood, and visiting other villages in the delta. Traditionally, mekoro are made from jackal-berry, marula, or sausage trees, as they invariably grow tall and straight and have a strong wood that is favourable for carving. The trees must be ancient, as they need to be tall for a more spacious hull.

A mokoro looks much like the punts typically found in Oxford and Cambridge. The poler will stand at the back and use a long, hardened pole to push the boat over the water, gliding through the swamp.

My poler pushed our mokoro away from the land and we glided into the vegetation-choked waters. Water lilies floated past with their bright white flowers opening up to the blue sky. African jacanas (also known as Jesus birds or lily-trotters) danced nimbly over the lilies, and storks elegantly moved through the water picking out food. We moved smoothly through the looking-glass still water watching small fish dart in and out of the vegetation and invertebrates clamour up the stems of plants from the water.

'River horses' (otherwise known as hippos) frequent the area too, and they were eating vast amounts of vegetation that clogged up the narrow channels and waterways. We could hear them calling in the long papyrus grass and snorting as they broke the water's surface.

It is a lazy way to experience the Okavango, and simply the best. Sitting there at eye level with the animals gives you a different perspective from higher in a vehicle, and as I trailed my fingers in the cool water and sat back in my chair I let myself be taken through the waterways without a care in the world.

There are a myriad of insects and small invertebrates to see. As the mokoro finds its way through the water small insects are gently disturbed from their positions. It is an entomologist's delight watching the small, colourful spiders balloon off the edge of the mokoro in search of a more stable habitat, dragonflies manoeuvring between reeds, and butterflies flitting carelessly across the water's surface. I could even see emerald-green miniature frogs, the size of my thumbnail, clinging to plant stems about 20cm above the water. I felt as if I was in Lilliput from *Gulliver's Travels*.

Just before we returned to our camp I saw a herd of elephants splashing in the water, sending liquid rainbows into the sky as they hauled out the waterlilies to eat. I was amazed at how close we got, we parked up about 30m away from them and simply sat and watched these wonderful animals going about their business. I could hear the content rumblings as the elephants communicated with each other and the constant sloshing of the water as they gradually moved through the swamp. The contrast of the iridescent-green water lilies, the bright blue sky, and the elephants was truly magical.

Alternatively, you can go on safari by boat, giving you a more elevated view and a completely different perspective.

A few days later we were enthusiastically welcomed aboard our riverboat by Lyn, one of the Angels (women guides) at *Chobe Game Lodge*, the only game lodge in Botswana, (and maybe Africa for that matter), which has an all-female guide team. It's a marketing ploy, and a very good one.

Before we cast off, all of us were sitting comfortably in our camp chairs with a chilled glass of wine in hand. There were only five of us on this game-viewing boat, which gave us plenty of opportunity to move around to see the wildlife from the best angle.

We cruised up-river for a while watching carmine

bee-eaters flit in and out of the mud banks, crocodiles silently slip into the water, fish eagles calling from their high perches, and skittish antelope coming down to the water's edge to drink. The occasional snorting of hippos amongst the lilies completed the ambience. It was bliss.

We turned and drifted back downstream, past the lodge, towards a couple of mud banks in the river which were beginning to show a bit of wildlife activity as the day cooled and animals came out of the searing sun to drink at the water's edge. We had the best seat in the house for an elephant extravaganza. This was obviously the place to mud-bathe, and several herds of elephants waded through a small section of the river to these mud banks. Smaller elephants had to swim, sometimes completely submerged in the water, and it was touching to watch the older elephants assist the smaller, and more vulnerable, youngsters.

Lyn deftly positioned the boat on the edge of the mud bank and cut the motor. We could hear the rumbling of passing elephants, which were only 5m away, the trumpeting of excited youngsters, and the sound of mud splattering on elephant skin. The smell was also extraordinary! From the way the elephants carried on with their ablutions, it appeared that they were not bothered by our presence in the least.

It is all too easy to humanise: the delight of the youngsters in experiencing their mud bath; the pleasure of the older elephants as they majestically flung mud over themselves; the curiosity of those watching us on the boat; and the squeal of distress as an elephant calf was briefly separated from its mother.

I don't think there is anywhere else in Africa that

you can be certain to see so many elephants behaving in such a relaxed way, and so up-close and personal. We sat back to watch the elephants on parade – with a G&T in one hand, and a chicken wing snack in the other. My kind of game watching!

Swimming with Whale Sharks

Mozambique is a great place to snorkel, and an even better place to scuba dive. The coral reef is spectacular and you can see clown fish (the real-live Nemo's) swimming amongst the colourful corals, or sea fans at great depths, and even manta rays at 'cleaning stations' (areas in the sea that are a bit like a car wash). A manta ray will approach a cleaning station with its mouth open to indicate that it is ready for cleaning (and that it is safe for other fish to approach), and smaller fish, such as cleaner shrimps, wrasse, and gobies, will come along and remove parasites from the ray's skin and gills, on the mutual understanding that they will not get eaten.

I have been on a dive when I could have sworn that I saw a great white shark, and even the instructor had rather larger eyes than normal. I remember her indicating that we needed to dive deeper to get out of potential harm's way. I have seen manta rays with spans of over 4m and squadrons of devil rays swimming over us like planes in World War Two.

The fish here are curious and not scared of divers, which permits incredible sightings of all kinds of aquatic creatures ranging from powder blue surgeon fish, (so-called for their scalpel-like spines either side of the tail), to red-toothed triggerfish which are blue all over and, funnily enough, have red teeth, although one wonders why they need them as they feed on plankton. There is the delightfully colourful lion fish, part of the scorpionfish family and aptly named as they have many of the world's most venomous species. They do have a sting, although not necessarily in their tail, made of sharp spines coated with venomous mucus. Despite this, lionfish are really pretty to look at, browny orange in colour with white, vertical stripes and delicate appendages that wave and float around them like a lion's mane, making them appear larger than they actually are.

My most memorable underwater sighting was of a whale shark which are actually classed as fish, despite their huge size. The longest confirmed individual was 12.65m, and the heaviest weighed more than 36 tonnes, although, unconfirmed claims report considerably larger ones.

Whale sharks have a distinctive pattern of spots all over, and around the globe this has spawned many names. In Mexico they are known as *pez dama* or *domino*. They are treated as a deity in Vietnam and called *Ca Ong*, which literally translates as *Sir Fish*. In Madagascar their name is *marokintana* meaning *many stars*. But I think the best name is from Kenya, where whale sharks are called *papa shillingi*, coming from their myth that God threw shillings upon the shark, which are now its spots.

These gentle giants of the sea swim slowly to the surface where they consume plankton and small fish on their long journeys through the oceans. Their massive body has white stripes and columns of white spots on a dark background and a narrow mouth that extends across the full width of its flattened head. Its eyes are small and set far forward to see approaching food.

Whale sharks are harmless to humans, and appear curious about us. As they are mostly seen on the surface of the ocean, divers and snorkelers can swim with these gentle creatures, which is a truly unforgettable experience! The only risk is being unintentionally struck by the shark's large tail fin.

The first time I saw whale sharks up-close was on a dive from Tofu, near Inhambane, which is about half way up the coast of Mozambique. We were looking for manta rays and had been told to keep an eye-out for whale sharks on the way out on our 45-minute ride to the dive site. This gave me lots of time to scan the sea, although this did prove difficult as it was choppy. I spent a fair bit of time concentrating on holding on and not being jettisoned overboard.

It was on the way back when we saw the whale shark, after a glorious dive to see manta rays at their cleaning stations. Our skipper saw the whale first, and gently eased off the throttle. We had been briefed that if one did surface we could get into the water with it and swim close by, but we were not to touch it. Touching the skin can damage it as humans can pass on chemicals that might affect the shark.

I was beside myself when we saw it, and with everyone-for-themselves I was fighting with fellow passengers to put on my snorkel and fins. Not very friendly I know, but for me this was one of my life goals, and no one was going to stop me!

I literally threw myself into the sea, in a most undignified fashion, got myself oriented, and stuck my head in the ocean. And there I was, swimming alongside a whale shark, watching this majestic beast glide leisurely past me as I frantically tried to keep pace with it. It didn't seem bothered by the gaggle of squealing humans flailing around nearby, it simply continued to swim up the coast.

I was so close to this enormous fish that it didn't seem to be real. I would never have touched it, but I was close enough to have done so. Taking a deep breath, I swam so that I was level with its eyes and I watched in fascination as it opened its large mouth to gulp in more plankton, it was truly mind-boggling. Its mouth looked to be the size of an average car, although I was in the water and size does get magnified... And then, with a flick of his tail, the whale shark dove into the depths of the sea leaving me floating on the surface watching it disappear into the blue abyss.

Tracking Lions and Hyenas

"See the lion tracks here?" asked Ocean as he pointed to the ground. "And see the hyena tracks there? It is following the lion. This lion is large. We are following them both."

"When were they here?" I asked.

"This morning," said Ocean.

"But it is this morning," I whispered, my eyes the size of dinner plates. It was only 7.15am. Ocean smiled knowingly, he meant 5am was morning.

That morning I had got up before sunrise, dressed in my warm clothes, had a quick cup of tea, and then set off with Ocean on my early morning walking safari. Ocean had given me a comprehensive brief as to how to walk in the bush (take it slowly), where to be at all times (behind him – which I had no problem with) and how to behave on seeing wildlife (stay silent). He had said all this while loading his rifle, which I admit, was both reassuring and nerve-wracking in equal measure. We were ready for anything... weren't we?

As we walked down the escarpment from Muchenje Lodge, Ocean explained to me his bushman background. His father had taught him from an early age how to trap animals, how to survive in the bush without water, what to eat, what was poisonous, and everything he needed to know about survival in the bush. It was absolutely fascinating.

Ocean taught me so many things. How to set a trap for an impala, and how to position it across the pathways that the impala use to get to and from water and feeding areas. How the locals make house bricks out of termite-mound mud. How only the giant and pied kingfishers hover above the water (other kingfishers don't hover). How lions will attack you if you run away and that you are more likely to survive if you stay facing the lion and don't make sudden movements and if you try to look bigger than you are. How to tell the different species of birds by the spoor (tracks) left behind. He told me where he went to school and how to catch fish *en masse* (using a poisonous tree). Most fascinating of all to me was the difference between hyena and lion spoor, and how to track them.

The lion tracks we saw today were enormous and Ocean said it was probably a male. The claw marks were not visible, whereas the claw marks were visible from the hyenas, although they were hard to spot amongst all the other signs on the ground. The main pad of a lion has three protuberances at the bottom whereas the hyena has only two. I had difficulty seeing them until I got my eye in and then I could differentiate the evidence of lions and hyenas easily. With this new-found awareness, I noticed tracks everywhere, which was disconcerting.

We followed the tracks at a slow and steady pace, partly along a dirt road and then into the bush as both lions and hyenas veered away from the open road.

We began to pick up pace, Ocean scanning the horizon while I glugged back water to relieve my thirst (but mostly my dry, nervous mouth).

We had been silent for ten minutes of tracking and were in tune with our surroundings. The air of expectancy between us was high, mingled with nervous energy and pure adrenalin.

Cautiously rounding a termite mound, a large panorama opened up before us. We eagerly scanned the bush for lions or hyenas, but today was not our day. However, we did spook a troop of baboons that that set off alarm calls reverberating through the bush. We would never see the lions or hyenas now.

The bush walk was an incredible experience and one I would thoroughly recommend. It was with a mixture of disappointment and utter relief that we ended our morning excitement, it was breakfast time and my stomach had been growling for a while.

I admit I was secretly pleased we hadn't caught up with the lions or hyenas, with all the water I had drunk I wasn't too sure how my bladder would have held up!

There are times where you don't necessarily have to go out on foot to track lion, they can pitch up at the most inconvenient time. I have had a lion prowling around my tent at night, whilst I was in Botswana, and I was so in need to go to the loo that I precariously peed in the porch area - there was no way I was going to the ablution block that was situated over 100m away!

I've also been stuck *in* an ablution block for a couple of hours as lions wondered around the campsite, oblivious of me wanting to go to back to bed.

And I have also heard the slurping of lions as they drank out of my washing-up bowl in Mana Pools National Park in Zimbabwe. They do like to keep me on my toes.

Many years ago, I arrived at Phinda Game Reserve in South Africa, fresh from the plane, and the first thing I heard was a low roar. The guys at the camp said that there was a male lion which had been prowling around at the back of the buildings for the past couple of nights. I was too exhausted from my journey to register fully what they had said. After going to the loo (there seems to be a bit of a theme here!), and being concerned about getting back to my room with all my limbs intact, we all went out, carefully, to see if we could find the lion.

There were five of us in a tight-knit group, one armed with a gun, another one with a spotlight. We moved cautiously, quietly hugging the walls like ninjas and tightly bound together as if we were stuck together with duct tape.

When the lion roared we stealthily approached,

and when the lion was silent we became statues. It was a bit of a modern take on Grandmother's Footsteps, only with rather more serious repercussions if Grandma spotted us.

He was near the out-buildings and he was enormous. He was calling and yawning and showing off his manly frame as well as his enormous canines. The spotlight was trained on him and he just sat there nonchalantly, his eyes glowing from the light, surveying *his* territory. After a while, I think he got a bit fed up with the spotlight on him and he gracefully got up, muscles rippling, and slowly moved off into the trees.

One does wonder what on earth I was thinking, but it was worth it. What a welcome to Africa, a special, exhilarating moment to remember.

Drive Across Etosha

Grab life by the horns, and drive yourself across Etosha National Park. Despite it only being about 160km from the Anderson Gate in the south west, to the Von Lindequist Gate in the east, it will take you all day. Etosha Pan was originally a lake that dried up millions of years ago. The park covers an area of 22,270km², and accommodates 114 species of mammal, 380 bird species, and 110 types of reptile. Surprisingly, perhaps, there are also 16 species of amphibians and even one fish to discover. It is one of Namibia's oldest national parks and was designated a protected area in 1907.

Today, I was driving west to east through the park and I was conscious of not making the rookie error of spending too much time in the western section and not leaving myself enough time to explore the eastern side. My day began with an early breakfast. You are required to hold a permit to get into Etosha and this is paid for at one of the three rest camps. There are brilliant maps of the area with the waterholes marked, showing whether they are borehole, (meaning that they have water in them all year), or whether they are natural and subject to drying out. The wonderful thing about self-driving is that you can get excited just by making a plan of which route to choose to cross the park. Of course, this will change with the incredible wildlife sightings that you might make, but I loved anticipating what I was going to see on my self-planned route.

I had made the decision to avoid the main camp of Okaukuejo and, instead, to wind my way directly to the first borehole on my route, Gemsbokvlakte. What a great decision this was. I think I was only the second car to stop on the gravel road beside a pride of eleven lions. What a treat! It was away from the waterhole and not many people had driven along this road that morning, so the bush telegraph hadn't had a chance to scare the animals away. I had the pride virtually to myself for half an hour.

The beauty of driving yourself is that you can stop and look at things for as long as you want and you don't get swept up by other people trying to bag as many animals as possible. I love taking Africa at a slow pace and allowing the surroundings to speak for themselves.

I watched a kori bustard walk past me, Africa's largest flying bird, although it is so large that it often doesn't bother taking to the air. It took ten minutes to pass me by because he was busy surveying his territory.

Practically all roads in Etosha are made of dirt, not tarmac, and there is a general speed limit of 60km/h. However, it is advisable to go slower than that as you never know what you might miss. I find that sometimes there seems to be an urgent rush to get from one waterhole to the next but there are so many other opportunities to see wildlife on the way that a slow, steady speed will enable you to see much more. I nearly drove past a black rhino once, and it was only 20m off the road in some light cover. If I had been driving any faster, I would certainly have missed it.

After seeing numerous elephants at waterholes, vast herds of gemsbok (large black and white antelope with straight pointed horns, also known as oryx), and a regal male lion, I decided to move on from the western part of Etosha to the Etosha Look-out. The roads to the Look-out simply go straight onto the Etosha Pan. The scenery is extraordinary, and it is like being on the moon - nothing but flat, white nothingness for miles and miles and miles, in complete contrast to the bright blue sky and the little marker posts that outline the 'road'.

On your Etosha permit the regulations say that you need to stay in the vehicle at all times, apart from at designated toilets, but it seemed that most people ignored this rule and got out of their car to enjoy the vast expanse of nothingness. I suppose you would be able to see a lion if it was approaching... but definitely not something to attempt in the bush!

It was now around lunchtime and, as I stopped at another waterhole keeping my eyes peeled to see if anything interesting would come along, I munched on my copious supplies of snacks. When you are driving in Namibia it is best to have a lot of water and an assortment of drinks on you. Think what you would normally drink, and then quadruple it, and, of course, lots of yummy snacks! I had slightly overdone it on the snack front and I think I had half a cow's worth of biltong.

The lovely thing about driving in Etosha is that you never really know what you will see around the next corner. I was lucky that day, I'd seen black rhinos, elephants, and lions. As I was driving along the roads that clung to the pan a flick of a tail caught my eye and there, in the shade of an acacia tree, lay three cheetahs. They were a distance away but I had these fantastic predators to myself and I could watch them at my leisure, as I chomped through my biltong.

Before I left the park, I decided to visit one more waterhole, Chudob. There were a few vehicles around the waterhole but generally fellow travellers are co-operative at making room for each other to get a good view, and the design of the park allows for a few vehicles to simply park and watch the wildlife extravaganza unfold.

As I approached I could see a number of giraffes drinking, and I excitedly got my camera out and clicked away. I was so busy looking at the giraffes I neglected to look around the rest of the waterhole.

Admittedly, they had been still, statue-like, but there was no excuse, I had nearly missed three hyenas lounging by the water's edge. I'd recently read an article about some clever hyenas that had learned to 'fish' in one of the waterholes and my luck was in. Motionless, crouching in the pan with its snout inches away from the water, sat a hyena waiting for lunch. It was remarkable, I've never seen anything quite like it before. I really wished I had a better lens on my camera, as I settled back with more biltong to see whether he was going to be successful. I watched him for an hour as he watched the water, and then he gave up on his fishing and laboriously hauled himself out of the water to dry in the heat. Not a lucky fishing expedition that time, maybe tomorrow.

What a day it had been, all nine hours of it. Yes, it had taken me nine hours to drive 160km. I had been lucky in my sightings, but even if I hadn't seen lions or hyenas, the scenery itself was extraordinary. You are practically guaranteed to experience a mini-adventure on a self-drive, whatever you come across. Now, where's my map? I need to get home.

Running the Gauntlet

I was out on foot tracking rhinos. There were four of us: Africa, our guide; Terry and Vicky, who were my guests; and myself. I love walking in the bush, you never know what you are going to see or who you are going to be walking with. The four of us set off into the unknown making sure that we were quiet and that we always knew where the good trees to hide behind were in case of charging rhinos or elephants.

I was bringing up the rear, making sure that the unexpected was expected and that no feisty elephants would sneak up on us. You may think that this is impossible, given their size, but an elephant's step is one of the quietest out there and it is surprising how you can lose an elephant in the bush, they blend in so well. But lose them you can.

There I was, giving the landscape the *Terminator* scan when, suddenly, looming over my right shoulder, was the head of an ostrich. (My *Terminator* scan was temporarily dysfunctional.) I have no idea where she came from, but there she was, walking behind me as if she was part of our party. She gave me a bit of a scare and I moved away from her pretty fast to ensure my body remained intact. Ostriches can disembowel a human if they want to. However, this one was more concerned with being part of our group than removing my innards.

At the time, Africa had been telling us about rhino poo and how a 'crash' of rhino (what a brilliant collective noun) will defecate in the same place and use it a bit like the Post Office to leave messages for one another. He had also been telling us about the numerous uses of elephant poo such as: insect repellent; a source of water (but only when in dire need); a mild painkiller; good for the sinuses; for making paper; as biogas; and even for a bizarre beer. It was at this point that the ostrich joined us, maybe she wanted to learn about elephant poo too!

Terry and Vicky had a good laugh at my sudden, erratic movements, until they realised the reason behind them. They then received the same scrutiny as I had, and this ended up with all of us trying to get away from her. She was none too pleased by this and she proceeded to herd us together, and neatly took over my job of bringing up the rear.

Ostriches are nosy creatures and will approach new objects, whether they be animal, vegetable, or mineral, to satisfy their curiosity. I am convinced that they have a short memory; their brain is smaller than their eye.

We were a strange group of animals walking through the bush, four humans and one ostrich. There are not many ostriches in Hlane, and I wondered whether she was just lonely and wanted some company. She stayed with us for twenty minutes, enjoying being part of our flock before moving off to find something more interesting to follow. She was a gentle ostrich with no other agenda.

However, there is one ostrich that used to scare the wits out of me regularly. The embarrassment of being chased by that bird makes me cringe, even today. Knowing that you've been chased by one of our feathered friends does not do much for your street cred, or rather bush cred.

The ostrich in question lives in Mbuluzi Game Reserve in Swaziland, and she gets rather protective and is particularly territorial. Unfortunately, the area she considers to be her domain is by the main gate and so getting out of your vehicle to open the gate becomes more of a challenge than a routine task. It is a bit like running the gauntlet, and the threat of physical damage is real. Whenever I approach the gate I find myself cautiously looking around for this elusive, insistent ostrich. If I have seen her earlier then I would know where she is and that would make things more manageable. However, if I have not seen her, life would become a little bit more adventurous and unpredictable.

Then there is the excitement of getting out of the car, opening the gates, getting back into the car, driving it through the gates, getting back out of the car, closing the gate behind you – all the while ensuring that all the right animals are on the correct side of the fence.

On this day, she *was* in the vicinity. In fact it appeared as if she was guarding the gates as she was walking up and down the entrance area like a sentry. Things could turn ugly. As I drove closer she eyeballed me showing her intent not to move. I gingerly got out of the car, and waved my arms frantically at her to get her to move, which she obligingly did with a big flutter of her wings. However, she just moved around the car and what ensued was a comedy moment between woman and ostrich. I kept running around the car waiting for a gap so I could open the gates without letting the ostrich escape from the reserve. I had parked my car as close to the 4½m-high gate as possible, just enough room so I could drive through. Eventually, she moved away a little bit so that I could open the gates and perform the car manoeuvre, this time with frenetic speed.

Luckily for me, she only made her dash for freedom at the last possible moment after I had driven through the gate. Although ostriches are pretty quick on this occasion I was faster. We were on a collision course, but I managed slam shut the gates before impact. She stopped just a few centimetres from me, wings outstretched and mouth agape, and if she was trying to intimidate me (which she had). I was glad that there was wire mesh between us.

Then there was a time when there was no wire

mesh between myself and another ostrich, and I was on foot. She was inexplicably away from her local hunting ground, probably she had gone for a little bit of a wander.

I was with a group of four volunteers, Jack, Flo, Anna, and Jon and we were surveying the vegetation in Mbuluzi Game Reserve to help the managers look at the carrying capacity of the land. On a map we had divided the reserve into $250m^2$ plots and were visiting each one to determine the dominant trees and bushes, and the average height of the grass It meant a lot of walking into the bush on a compass bearing and counting your steps to get into the middle of each imaginary square. It was a pleasure walking around in the bush as we never knew what we would encounter: wildebeest, zebra, giraffe, marauding ostriches.

As we emerged from the bush and onto one of the many dirt roads that crisscrossed the reserve, we spied her meandering near our vehicle, this was not looking good. The vehicle was a bakkie, a small two-seater truck with an open space in the back for others to sit. We had finished the survey work for the day, otherwise we would have ignored her and carried on back into the bush to sample the next plot. We were about 100m away from the bakkie, (our escape back to camp), and the ostrich, (our potential demise). Frankly, the odds weren't looking great.

Initially, we walked as a group towards the vehicle in the hope that the ostrich was having an off day and wouldn't have a go at us. Unfortunately, this was not the case and she looked keenly at us, large wings unfurled, mouth open, and eyes giving the death stare.

Anna was the first to bottle it and she veered off into the bush using trees as camouflage. Actually, she did really well and got to the bakkie. No doubt she felt pretty good sitting in the front of the vehicle! The ostrich still had its beady eye on the rest of us and was now 50m away from us and the vehicle. Jack peeled off next but she was not having any of it, and herded him back to the group. This was going to be tricky.

We came up with a cunning plan; Jack, Flo and Jon would stay as a group near to the road, distracting the ostrich with lots of movement and noise, while I surreptitiously went to the vehicle and drove back along the road, passing the ostrich, to collect them. Surely the ostrich wouldn't attack the vehicle?

The plan went well, I managed to weave, duck, and dive my way through the bush, got to the vehicle where I briefly acknowledged Anna's bravery, and then proceeded to drive the vehicle towards the other three. I gave the ostrich a wide berth, masses of space so as not to upset it, and I smiled as we chugged past the enormous bird. But, as I accelerated to get to Jack, Flo and Jon, the ostrich decided we were fair game and it broke into a slow trot after the vehicle. At this point the other three realised the problem and were already on the road ready to pile into the back of the vehicle. There was a mass of clambering as they threw themselves into the back and then a "Go! Go! Go!", and banging on the roof of the cab.

I needed no further encouragement. I floored the vehicle and sped off down the track. I think ostriches like to chase something and this was obviously what she had in mind. With the screams of the three students shouting hysterically, "Faster! Faster!

FASTER!" I belted along the track with a focused ostrich picking up speed behind us. I could see all of this in my mirrors. The needle on the speedumeter reached 40km/h and the ostrich was still there, now it got even closer, the students were flattened up against the cab, banging even louder on the roof to encourage me to go faster. Meanwhile, the ostrich was busy pecking at the tailgate. *Surely it would run out of steam at some point* I thought, *what sort of creature is this?*

We got to a small hill in the reserve and rocketed up this gravel track, stones spewing out all over the place, and it was only when we got to the top that I realized that we had out run our quarry.

The relief on everybody's faces said it all, yes, we had been run out of town by a bird.

Prickly Porcupines

"Would you like to go on a night drive, or visit the night hide?"

I was having a truly scrumptious meal at Okonjima Bush Camp, Namibia. There were only seven of us around the table and the camp provides a wonderfully genuine bush experience, with the added bonus of being able to go and visit a night hide. I immediately jumped at the opportunity because I had been told that often you could see porcupines and honey badgers. It had been a long time since I'd seen a porcupine and I thought going to the hide would round off a spectacular day nicely. Earlier on in the afternoon I had been on a game drive and had seen both leopards and cheetahs, so I was feeling lucky.

Only three of us decided to go to the hide and we

were told to come to reception in half an hour, so I had enough time to get back to my room and get my camera. My room was the furthest from the main part of the camp and wonderfully situated in the bush. Each room had a bed that faced out into the bush and mosquito netting protected you from curious visitors. At night, you could still see the stars twinkling in the big, clear sky. There was also my very own lounge area with numerous books for me to look up what I'd seen that day.

The three of us piled into the vehicle. On the way we saw giraffes and kudu, heard numerous birds, and were even treated to a mongoose disappearing into the undergrowth.

The hide looks out over a flat area, like a natural amphitheatre, surrounded by a rocky outcrop. We had brought a few leftover vegetables that we scattered on the 'stage' and we settled down to wait. I anticipated that it might be some time before we would see anything at all. I was so wrong.

Within minutes, there was a rustling in the bushes and a porcupine appeared from stage left. It was enormous! People are often surprised at how large porcupines are, but this one even surprised me. He was closely followed by his mate and we all held our breath so as not to spook them. I watched in awe as they settled down to the serious business of eating butternut skin and the remains of some lettuce. The air was still and I could hear every single crunch, snort, and gnaw they made. You could even hear their quills clanking together as they changed position to get the best angle on their food. It was mesmerising.

After the mum and dad had settled down, a

youngster appeared who had obviously learned the tricks of the trade from its parents. The juvenile was more wary of his surroundings, but eventually it also settled down to eat away through the delicious snack on offer.

We spent about an hour watching the animals. It is amazing how something as simple as watching porcupines feeding can make you appreciate the good things in life.

I admit I was rather pleased when we decided to leave, because we were not the only critters in the hide. The rains were beginning to bloom on the horizon and you could feel the build-up and tension in the area each day. This affects all kinds of creatures, one in particular that is my number one least favourite creature – the sun spider.

Solifugae is an order of animals in the class *Arachnida* known variously as camel spiders, wind scorpions, sun spiders, or solifuges. They are the ugliest creatures imaginable and I have an intense dislike of them. They are halfway between a spider and a scorpion with biting mouthparts that open horizontally and vertically. They have two big beady eyes, are more often orange or grey in colour, move towards light and movement, and generally give me the heebie-jeebies. Basically, they are one of the more primitive forms of wildlife and they make me shudder just writing about them.

Unfortunately, as we were sitting watching the porcupines, I noticed one scuttling across the floor behind one of the other guests, and I was not best pleased. This one was not particularly large; its body was only 5-6cm long. I have seen larger ones in

Zimbabwe and the really big ones can bite through a little finger. I wasn't about to put this theory to the test.

Sun spiders do not stay on the ground, they climb everything and anything, including trouser legs, chairs, and table tops. They are busy creatures, never staying still, and where there is one, there are normally a lot more. Not even watching porcupines was going to encourage me to stay for much longer.

My excitement didn't end there. On our return to the lodges, I was driven to my remote accommodation and, as the vehicle pulled up, we spotted an animal near the small lantern outside my room. I couldn't believe my eyes, it was an aardwolf – very rare indeed. Aardwolves are long-haired grey animals with four or five transverse white stripes on their flanks and a few stripes on their legs. They have large, pointy ears and a mane of long, dark hair running along their sloping backs. They are around 50cm high and the size of a Labrador, but one that has been on a diet. Their faces are sharp and pointy, with a dark muzzle and eyes, and they have a dark, bushy tail. They are part of the hyena family and their diet is protein-rich as they spend most of their night scoffing up termites with their broad, sticky tongue.

It just so happened that on that night the termites were flying out of a nest in order to expand their territory. This had attracted the aardwolf for his midnight snack. I tried to get a photograph of him but it wasn't good... but I at least I have the memory of seeing him.

HEARING

I was guiding visually-impaired guests around Africa. When I tell friends about this their immediate response is "How on earth does that work?" I admit that initially this was my response when I was creating their itinerary.

When I thought about it I realised that to me the essence of Africa is the sound of a honking hippo, the smell of the hard-baked earth, the feel of the warm sun caressing my face, and watching a young elephant running towards the water hole whilst I'm sipping my sundowner drink. Africa has so many wonderful sensory experiences that bring a smile to my face: the solitary call of the fish eagle; the whoop of hyenas at the quietest time of night; the bray of zebras echoing across the savannah; and the delicate popping noises that reed frogs make before rain.

There are many sounds of Africa that resonate with me, and what follows are some of those evocative sounds.

Cicada Cacophony and other African Sounds

If there was an Olympic event for the animal that can create the most noise in relation to its size, the cicada would easily get the gold medal. Cicadas produce the loudest insect sound in the world at 106.7 decibels at a distance of 50cm, which is similar to that of a power saw.

Trying to see one is a completely different kettle of fish. On approaching one by sound, the insect will suddenly go silent and leave its neighbours to continue with the cacophony, thus confusing you in the process. If you have children that you want to keep occupied for ages, give them the challenge of capturing a cicada!

After a while you will probably become so familiar with the loud, pulsating, incessant, deafening drone of cicadas that you will eventually become oblivious to it. Bizarrely, when it is not there it is sorely missed and it can make you suspicious, and slightly nervous as to why they are suddenly so quiet. Is there a large, angry predator in the bush? Is there a python slithering along the ground? Or, is there a rainstorm approaching? You never know, and at these times it feels as if the cicadas are the night watchmen of an unknown peril.

For me, the honk and snort of the hippopotamus is the epitome of the sound of Africa. This is probably because my first five days of being in the African bush was in the company of a pod of twenty-two hippos. Throughout the day, they honked and hawed at each other having what sounded like long and in-depth discussions. Hippos also have the unique ability to communicate in air and water; they can send out a honk that travels through both mediums resulting in hippos in and out of the water responding. It was like having an orchestra playing just for me, and it was a privilege to be there. Whenever I hear a hippo it heightens that feeling of excitement and contentment that I associate with being in Africa.

The eeriest call is that of the hyena. It is also known as the 'laughing hyena' because their chatter sounds like a human laughing hysterically. It is the 'whoop' that I love the sound of most. It is a call that can be heard from far away and is used by parents to find their cubs, claim territory, or bring the clan together. Often a hyena whoop can be heard in the still of the night, making it a chilling sound, particularly when you hear it in more remote settings than in the busier lodges, and even more so when you are in the bush with just canvas to protect you.

I remember camping at Sudwini campsite in Hlane National Park in Swaziland and we were in a section of the park that people don't often visit. The campsite is in a beautiful area on the edge of a dam where there was supposed to be a hippo pod. I hadn't actually heard a hippo at that time, but they were meant to be in the area, and this was the reason why I was up at 1.15am. There was a group of us and we were sleeping out under the stars in our bedrolls. Actually, they were much more than just a bedroll; inside each canvas roll was a plush mattress with sheets, a pillow and a lovely, thick, warm rug. All you had to do was to unzip the bedroll and climb into your portable bed.

Our bedrolls were laid out in rows like sardines in a can, on a canvas sheet, and underneath a temporary awning. I was at one end, so I could see the African stars twinkling above me as I lay in my sumptuous bed.

Unfortunately, I was not in it for long as my turn on the hippo-watch rota was at 12.30am. Hippos in the area occasionally walked through the camp at night and it was always a good idea to have someone on lookout in case this happened. The person responsible had a torch and his or her job was to sit by the fire, drink tea, and occasionally check the surrounding area for night-walking hippos. In the unlikely event that a hippo did come into the camping area it was that person's responsibility to calmly wake everybody up, move them aside, and quietly allow the hippo to walk through. It was unlikely, but not out of the question...

There I was, sipping my tea and warming my hands in front of the embers of a wonderful, glowing fire. There were the gentle sounds of the night: the chirp of a bat as it flew overhead; the gentle buzz of a cricket; and the distinctive call of a fiery-necked nightjar singing 'Good Lord deliver us'. It was magical.

It was not a hippo that broke the calm, but a brief screech that pierced the night air. This was the unmistakable yelp of a black-backed jackal, and then everything settled back into its natural rhythm once again.

Shortly afterwards, hyenas joined the night orchestra, with their mournful whoop from somewhere in the distance, beautifully blending into the night chorus. Their call is a rounded 'oo' tone, which begins in a low pitch and ends with a high note, whilst gently going up the scale. It is usually made up of a series of 6–9 calls lasting 2–3 seconds each and spaced 2–10 seconds apart. This sound can be heard more than five kilometres away and you wait in anticipation for the next solo act. This call never fails to cause the hairs on the back of my neck to tingle. It is a beautiful, melodious sound that makes me feel contented. While many people would feel fearful, knowing what a hyena can do, it doesn't have this effect on me.

I always feel I need to stick up for the poor, maligned hyena. *The Lion King* has got a lot to answer for in giving them such a bad name. They are often depicted as scavenging, bloodthirsty animals that steal unsuspecting lions' well-earned kill. Yes, they might be scavengers and often there are pictures of them with unattractive, bloody faces but statistics show that lions are much more likely to steal a hyena's kill than vice versa. The fact that the lion is part of the 'Big Five' and the hyena is part of the 'Ugly Five' does not help the hyenas' case.

The Big Five refers to five large mammals found in Africa: lions, leopards, elephants, rhinoceroses, and cape buffalos. Why not hippopotamuses, or giraffes – they are big aren't they? The hippo certainly is. The reason for the Big Five tag is that these five animals were the hardest to shoot by big-game hunters as they are particularly ferocious when cornered and injured. Tour operators and guides have picked up on the phrase and used it as a marketing term that has stuck despite the hunting origin.

I think it is a real shame that the 'Ugly 5' have been given this label, and not something to be proud of. They are the underdogs of the African plains and hold just as important a role as any of the other African animals. The members of this club are: hyenas, wildebeest, vultures, warthogs, and marabou storks. There are numerous documentaries about the antics, the migration, and the unusual habits of these species so these animals are certainly worth a tick in the book.

Whenever I return to Africa I realise that I have missed these sounds terribly, although I don't realise it until I hear them again. When I do, I become awash with that feeling of belonging, a feeling of happiness, a feeling for Africa.

Birdhearing in Africa

I am excited because I have just got *Roberts' Multimedia Birds of Southern Africa*. Now I can listen to the calls of African birds and try to commit them to memory whilst eating my breakfast.

Until I went to Africa, I was never really interested in birds. My mum has always been fascinated by them, and she can hear a bird song and easily identify it. When I was young, I remember spending ages looking for the right kind of bird bath for her birthday so she could see the birds from the kitchen window: it still sits in my parents' garden so I must have got the right one. I did get a bit excited about seeing birds in the bird bath, but most of those found in the UK are drab by comparison to their African cousins. At times their migratory relations do visit the UK, but it's rare for the more colourful ones to get blown off course and visit our shores.

In contrast, African birds are gloriously-coloured, often have some quirky nature to them, and are relatively easy to identify. They also have the most extraordinary songs, glorious songs that fill the African bush, and at times it is much easier to find a bird by song rather than by sight.

After my first visit to Africa I became hooked on birding, becoming a bit of a twitcher myself – something of which I am now proud. It also makes those local visitors to my parents' bird bath seem less tedious as I appreciate them so much more now.

Most people who visit Africa also get the bug and spend increasingly longer periods of time poring over bird books in an attempt to identify all manner of avifauna. These might have been sighted whilst out on a game drive, heard during breakfast, or spotted whilst sitting overlooking a waterhole as the sun sets. The latter is best done with a your choice of tipple, if you want to take a more relaxed approach to birding.

Despite people calling it bird 'watching', it's more like bird 'hearing'. Once you familiarise yourself with the calls of the various species it becomes easier to know what you're looking for, and where to find them, which makes it less frustrating to spot them.

For instance, the crested barbet has a distinctive, if monotonous, territorial call. This sound punctures the bush with its staccato, machine-gun trill. I remember the first time I identified this bird's call. I was staying in Mlilwane Wildlife Reserve in Swaziland, and every morning, without fail, this little bird woke me with its incessant song. I became determined to find out who the culprit was. Eventually, after following the sound in ever-decreasing circles, I found the bird perched on top of a fence post, singing its little heart out in the African morning. It is stunning to look at (if not so pleasant to listen to) – a yellow and red speckled face with a black crest on the top of its head and a bright, yellow chest with a black band. *Roberts'* says its call is '...an unmusical trill, likened to an alarm clock with the bell removed.' I concur.

The fish eagle also possesses an easily identifiable call. It is a plaintive and heart-rending cry that travels for miles over the treetops. Once you know that it is a fish eagle calling, it is easier to see the bird, as you know that you are looking for its white bib, which is strikingly obvious in the trees surrounding the lakes and waterholes it frequents. There is a pair in Mlilwane, Swaziland, which are often seen by the main dam and their distinctive white chests give them away from afar. It is the first place that I head for on arriving in Swaziland. I often stop on the dam road to see whether I can spot them. Of course, their call is distinctive and whenever I hear it a huge smile appears across my face. The call of the fish eagle brings with it a sense of well-being.

To get a great sighting of the fish eagle a river cruise on the Chobe River in Namibia is the ideal location. These magnificent birds are often seen majestically perching on prominent branches as they survey their territory and occasionally swoop down to catch fish, which are then carried back to the perch or dragged to shore if too big to carry. I've seen one take a poor, unsuspecting duck. African fish eagles also eat birds, monkeys, and crocodile hatchlings. These highly-efficient predators can get away with spending as little as ten minutes a day actively hunting.

They don't often move but when they call they arch their heads behind until they just about touch their back, and then they project their haunting call by throwing their head forward. An awful lot of effort is put into this cry and it is fascinating to watch.

The bee-eater delights the eye: a gloriously colourful bird with striking features and lovely to watch. But, it has an ugly call that does not match its beauty. The call sounds like an old barn door stubbornly opening, and is positively grating on the ear. To see this bird, you should look for the prominent branches from which it hunts, or in the air as it catches insects on the wing.

The chinspot batis is a tiny bird, adorned with black and white markings. The female has a bold chinspot and a broad, chestnut-coloured breast-band, whereas the male simply has the broad breast band in black. They can both be difficult to spot. However, their call comprises of three notes, reminiscent of 'Three Blind Mice', once heard, never forgotten, and provides a distinctive aural signpost for a visual spotting.

Weaver birds build the most extraordinary nests, taking care, time, and patience to achieve what I consider to be a most impressive feat of construction. They build the most elaborate nests of all birds: they are nature's engineers. The males build the nest, then the females come in at the last moment to give them the seal of approval, or not as the case may be.

First, a male finds a suitable collection of branches for their new home. The nest must hang in a well-ventilated place, safe from marauding snakes, and built to perfection. Normally, two or three branches are tied together to form the basis of the nest – I'd liken this task to tying your shoelaces with your mouth. Then, strands of grass, individually chosen, are woven around the branches to form a nest in the shape of a carafe of wine. It takes the male weeks to

85

build, making up to 500 trips to collect suitable blades of grass, whilst the female critically watches his every move.

Once the nest is ready, the female comes to inspect it. If it is not to a suitable standard she will destroy the whole thing while the male looks on in bewilderment. He must start all over again, building the new one to a higher standard. Sound familiar?

And then there is the sound of thousands of birds in one place. Take the gigantic flocks of red-billed queleas, the most abundant wild bird species, which have an estimated adult population of 1.5 billion. Yes, that's billion, it's not a typing error. I find that too many to compute. They are similar to a finch and the males look like they've dunked their head in red paint. They are uninspiring birds individually, but as a flock they are a force to be reckoned with.

I saw these birds when I was living in Zimbabwe. An enormous flock, that blotted out the sun, arrived and began nesting in the *Save Valley Conservancy*. Thousands upon thousands of small birds making nests in any tree that they could find. The noise was truly deafening. Vegetation from miles around was stripped bare for nesting materials and seeds and flowering plants were being decimated for food. It was an extraordinary spectacle. They moved like locusts, leaving a wake of destruction as they collectively chirped across the savannah. The conservancy area was hit hard as these marauders spent more time than usual in the area.

There were some species benefiting from this valuable food source, namely snakes and crocodiles. There were snakes galore in the area feeding on chicks that had inadvertently fallen out of their nests and also eggs from within. However, my most memorable experience was watching the crocodiles feeding on the quelea. They would remain just under the surface of the water and when the noisy birds came down to drink the crocodiles would launch themselves out of the water and snap up any unsuspecting bird. The crocodiles certainly got a few birds on each snap, but I wondered whether the energy used was worth the feathered popcorn bites that they got.

After a couple of weeks, this swarm of birds suddenly upped and left, leaving the bush in a state of bewilderment from their feathered onslaught. They left it a much quieter place than when they arrived.

Birdhearing is an art, and it is also relatively easy to pick up. However, it does take a bit of time to get in tune with the noises of the African bush, so give your ears a chance and before long you will find it easy to identify birds from their calls.

I'm going back to my newly-found acquisition so I can listen to the bird call of every single bird in southern Africa, with a host of other useful information to marvel at. Twitcher, signing off.

Hearing... Nothing

One of the great things about going to Africa is that you can leave modern communications behind, turn off your mobile phone, your laptop and iPad, and truly appreciate life here and now. Often lodges in Africa do not have electricity let alone Wi-FI; instead there are paraffin lanterns and hot water is produced by fire, solar power, or gas boilers. After a while you come to realise that electricity is not a necessity, just a luxury that we take for granted. Let your electronic appliances run flat and concentrate on re-charging your own batteries.

Once your tech is turned off you notice the difference – there are no aggravating beeps as text messages come through, no phones ringing, no muffled drum beat from someone's headphones, and no constant hum of a laptop. Instead, there is just the sound of nature. Funnily enough this can be unnerving to begin with but, over time, technology can be eliminated from your holiday, although for some this can be a painful withdrawal process. Bear with it, as it is only when you can't have something that you realise how addicted you are to it.

Nature can be noisy. In fact, it can be deafening. However, there are places in Africa where you can truly appreciate the peace and tranquillity of the wilderness and absolute silence.

I love spending a night on the salt pans – it's an out-of-this-world experience. Nothing seems real. Imagine spinning around and the view simply doesn't change at all, just a wide expanse of nothing. This is what it is like out on Makgadikgadi Pan in Botswana. There are few places in the world where you could describe the view as 'nothing', and the salt pans are just one such place.

You don't have to rough it to get the experience of being in the middle of nowhere. There are a number of places to stay – wonderful lodges in the middle of nowhere with a vast expanse of emptiness surrounding them.

It's inspiring, although initially many people find

it unnerving. However, my first experience of complete silence happened while I was on expedition, and the first time I spent a night out on Makgadikgadi Pan is still a fresh and wonderful memory.

We travelled in two vehicles. I was in the one at the rear and I learnt from this schoolgirl mistake and logged it for the future. The dust from the vehicle in front often prevented me from keeping my eyes open, and my face at the end of the day looked as if I was wearing a white clay mud mask. Despite this I could still spot the odd ground squirrel scampering for cover and a couple of lone jackals searching for something tasty to eat in the harsh environment. There was also an eagle circling in the sky waiting for some hapless creature to succumb to the searing heat that bounced off the white ground. The vegetation diminished as we travelled closer to the salt pans until there was little more than grass – grass that was yellow and had negligible hope of surviving to the next month.

The horizon expanded even more, and I am sure that I could see over the edge of the curvature of the Earth. The sky was full of wispy, zebra-tail clouds galloping across the sky, it would be a perfect night. The salt pan filled the horizon. A vast sea of white. Flat as a pancake and exceptionally difficult to discern how far you are looking – maybe it was 400 metres maybe it was 40 kilometres, I couldn't tell. There was nothing to gauge distance.

Makgadikgadi is an area the size of Portugal and largely uninhabited by humans. Its stark, flat, featureless terrain seems to stretch to eternity, meeting and fusing with a milky-blue horizon. It is part of the Kalahari Basin and is one of the largest salt pans in the world. For much of the year most of this desolate area remains arid; and large mammals are absent. You may be lucky enough to see a random, solitary, brown hyena – a dark shape slinking across the white background. During, and following, years of good rain the largest pans flood, and this attracts wildlife such as zebra and wildebeest onto the newly-grassed plains.

As the vehicles slowed I noticed that as the lake had dried up it had left behind a superficial maze of enormous curling salt flakes about the size of large dinner plates, but not much else. We continued to drive on the pan and into 'nowhere', where we stopped for the night.

'Nowhere' was our planned destination; there were a few logs left behind from a previous visit and these were set alight, along with more firewood from the truck. A toilet was dug – a hole in the middle of nowhere with an awning erected around it. Not much to hide behind, but then there's not not much to hide from!

By now the fire was blazing and the aroma of sizzling steak being grilled over the braai (barbeque) made me drool like Homer Simpson. Chairs were set up around the fire in traditional mobile safari style and as I had my sundowner (a drink consumed at sunset) I watched the sun sink below the horizon. It was out of this world and the sun appeared to be larger, brighter, and redder than I had ever seen it before.

Tents are not needed here, it is one of the few wild places in southern Africa where you can sleep out under the stars without fear of an unwanted slithery guest in your sleeping bag, or an attack from scavenging animals. A roll mat and your torch will suffice.

After supper I picked up my sleeping kit and tentatively ambled out into the void of Makgadikgadi Pan. I had an uneasy feeling that I would come across something scary and nobody would be there to help save the day. I felt vulnerable as the light of the fire finally diminished into a small speck behind me.

It was a surreal experience as I walked into the vastness of the salt pan. I felt insignificant and totally reliant on my own abilities – which was unnerving. I challenged myself to walk as far away from the fire and my fellow human beings as I possibly could, to enjoy the solitude and to be at one with the environment. I willed myself not to look back at the campfire until I was sure I'd walked a considerable distance. When I had done this, and then walked a little bit more, I looked back at the fire to gauge how far away I was from it. I had no idea how far away I was but to me, it was far enough. It seemed an acceptable distance, so I set up my own little camp of my roll mat, a sleeping bag and my backpack.

The wind on the pans tends to pick up in the evening and many a roll mat has been lost into the distance never to be seen again and resulting in a rather uncomfortable night. My bag also acted as a good windbreak and stopped sand and salt kicking up into my face during the night.

Why was I doing all of this, I hear you ask? Well... why not? It is not often you get the chance to sleep literally in the middle of nowhere, to have the peace and tranquillity of Africa wrapped around you, and the knowledge that you are safe. It takes some guts as it is the fear of the unknown that ties you to the fire but, once your fear is stretched, (or even broken), it is a remarkable experience. I had a great night's sleep, although I admit I was a bit twitchy to begin with. Complete silence can be disconcerting. I did occasionally hum to myself to ensure that I had not gone deaf.

When I woke up the following morning, I was mortified to find that I was only 150m away from the fire! It had felt like I had walked at least a kilometre the previous evening.

When was the last time you slept and only heard your own breathing? Shut your eyes when you go to bed next, and listen to your environment – you're sure to hear *something*. True silence can be deafening.

"What Was That?" <scared voice>

Did you know that a lion's roar can be heard over 8km away? That is a considerable distance for a mammal to project, and the sound that you hear is nothing like the lion roaring at the beginning of the *MGM* films – that is the voice of a severely hacked-off lion.

The Swazis (unsurprisingly from Swaziland) impersonate the sound of a lion very well whilst saying "Who's the king? Who's the King? Me, me, me." This always makes me smile. I think I can also make a decent impersonation by sticking my head into a large saucepan to create what I think is the ideal lion-roar resonance.

The roar of a lion vibrates through your body and,

even if you haven't heard one before, when you do you can immediately identify it. The hairs on your neck will stand up, your heart rate will increase, and your brain will kick into gear to tell you in no uncertain terms that this is definitely a lion you can hear.

I vividly remember the first time I heard a lion roar. I was camping in Zimbabwe without any prior real-world experience of the sound of a lion. Of course, I'd seen them on the TV, but never experienced it in real life – not even in a zoo or wildlife park. When I heard it I knew exactly what it was. I was concerned for the safety of the people who were with me, (and for me too!).

My friend Keith was working in Gonarezhou National Park in Zimbabwe, and lions were common as muck there, so when I called him to ask what to do, he flippantly replied, 'Put out a saucer of milk.' Not particularly helpful Keith, thanks.

The best place to hear lions roar is when you're in bed, tucked up safely. No, really, I've been lulled to sleep by the soporific call of a lion. However, if this is the first time that you've heard a lion roar, you may find yourself lying there wide-eyed and white-knuckled with a death grip on your sheets for the rest of the night.

Being on foot in the bush can be terrifying, as well as exhilarating. It is a strange mixture and yet I love it. Never has the gentle rustling in the undergrowth and the sharp cracking of twigs caused so much fear in a person, especially with the knowledge that there are white rhinos and elephants nearby. And this is where I found myself for five days of intense survey work. I was doing some ecological data collection to look at the impact of elephants on the trees in Hlane, Swaziland.

Elephants love the taste of bark and will tear sheets of this protective layer off the trees as a tasty snack. The issue is that if all the bark is removed in a complete ring around the circumference of the tree, the tree will die. The bark consists of cork cambium, phloem, cambium, and sometimes even the xylem, and these all make up the complex transfer system that takes sugars from the leaves to the roots, and water and minerals from the roots to the leaves.

It was evident, by looking at the trees, that the impact of the elephants had been catastrophic. Twisted skeletons of acacia trees stood solemnly on the horizon painting a bleak picture. It would be our detailed information that we would collect that would prove to be important to show which species were being hit the worst. It would also establish the status of the remaining food options for these elephants.

Dumi, our Ranger, was with us for the survey work and kept an eye out for the elephants and rhinos in the area. He is one of the best rangers in the park, although I was wondering what would happen if an elephant did charge as he only carried a large, polished stick with a bulbous part at one end. He also had a radio, but no water, no food, and no gun. I suspect that Dumi was probably rather amused by our antics in the bush. He seemed to glide effortlessly through the vegetation where I and the three volunteers got ourselves hooked, scratched, and impaled by every sharp pointy thing in the vicinity.

I found myself, in a particularly dense thicket of thorny bushes, attempting to walk in a straight line whilst noting down the species of trees around me and whether they were dead or alive. At that point of the day it had been rather tedious. I, and the other volunteers who were helping me, had walked about 2km and had identified 53 trees, most of which were dead, and we were covered in scratches. We were hot and tired and in need of some alternative entertainment.

It was also nerve-wracking trying to extricate yourself from these bushes, which seemed to have magnetic properties, whilst maintaining minimal noise in the process. We needed to keep our senses alert for elephants and rhinos. You would have thought it would be easy to see such big animals coming a mile off; however they have the amazing ability to blend into their environment, especially rhinos as, during the middle of the day, they often lie down, making them even more camouflaged and easy to stumble upon.

I didn't hear the movement in the vegetation up front, but Dumi had. He gestured for all of us to be quiet. We froze like we were playing musical statues, held our breath, and waited. It seemed like we waited for an eternity but then we all heard the gentle cracking of dried twigs and branches and the soft snort of nostrils against the earth – there be rhinos ahead! At this point we could only hear them, but not see them, highlighting the importance of using your hearing whilst you are in the bush. Dumi waved us over to him with hand movements that meant, 'Keep it quiet.'

Rhinos have incredible hearing, it is one of their keenest senses. Their eyesight is rubbish and, if you are downwind of a rhino and remain absolutely still and as quiet as a mouse, a rhino can walk towards you oblivious of your presence. It can be standing around 10m away, and they still won't know you are there. I know this, it has happened to me.

However, you certainly do not want to spook them as they can be erratic in the direction of their escape route!

As quietly as possible, we extricated ourselves from the vegetation and slowly and quietly made our way over to Dumi. There, only 20m away, sat two rhinos in limited shade from the midday sun. They were resting on their bellies with their feet tucked in under them, their giant heads resting on the ground and the occasional snort coming from their enormous nostrils sending a flurry of dust swirling into the air. Oxpecker birds flitted around them, feeding off the numerous ticks that had attached to the rhinos' thick hide. Their ears twitched, listening to the sounds of the bush, alert to danger or for anything unusual. They looked like satellite dishes collecting all the sound waves in the area; it was wonderful to watch.

Then the ear-twitching stopped and one of the two rhinos abruptly sat up – alarmingly quickly considering its – size, its head swaying from side to side. This caused the other one to respond and it got to its feet in one fluid motion, tail and head up sniffling the air while its ears scanned its surroundings.

Dumi motioned for us to stay where we were, and he took a few steps towards the rhino, which at the time I thought was a pretty ridiculous choice from the options available. He slowly bent down and casually tapped the ground in front of him with his long stick. The rhino heard this, stopped moving and squinted in his direction. Dumi casually tapped the ground again ensuring that he had the full attention of both rhinos, which he now did. These two enormous white rhinos stood facing Dumi, both gently swaying from side to side, and all Dumi had was a stick. We stood only 3m from Dumi. The whole situation was ludicrous. It would have made a great photo but I certainly hadn't the presence of mind to even think along that line at the time.

Then, the rhinos casually turned around and trotted away, crashing through the bushes making a horrific amount of noise as they hurrumphed while running. It might seem a bit of an anti-climax but I was relieved at the outcome. Dumi turned around with a massive smile on his face, he had obviously loved the whole experience. I was thrilled at that moment, although a few seconds earlier if I had opened my mouth he might have seen my heart thumping away inside. I turned around to see similar expressions on the faces of the volunteers. The remaining few hours of survey work had an air of anticipation as we kept our hearing on high alert for any unusual noises to warn us of rhinos or elephants.

Over the years, I have become accustomed to the noises of the bush and their nuances, so when I hear something abnormal my senses immediately kick into high-alert status. A valuable commodity when you spend a lot of time walking in the bush.

Tracking Desert Rhino in Damaraland

"I will give you a wake-up call at 5.30am," said Bons, "and let you know if it is safe to come over to breakfast, or if I need to escort you."

He waited for my reaction. Well, it was quite early, but I was expecting this. There were a few wild animals knocking around and I didn't particularly fancy being anybody's early morning snack.

"Brilliant," I responded, to which Bons raised an eyebrow and gave me a smile. He was obviously used to people complaining about getting up early or about the dangerous animals.

I was staying at Desert Rhino Camp in the heart of Damaraland, north-west Namibia, and I was being briefed by Bons, my guide, about how the following day was going to pan out. I was also learning about the importance of the work that *Save the Rhino Trust* undertakes in the area. I couldn't believe how vast the concession was, and it was here that the largest free-roaming, desert-adapted, black rhino population in Africa resides. Now, that is certainly something to be proud of. Our goal tomorrow was to see whether we could spot any of these elusive animals.

5.30am came around far too quickly. Bons told me that it was safe to walk from my tent to the communal area, so I got ready quickly for the day and made my way over to where breakfast was being served. My 'tent' was enormous and plush inside, and I had struggled to get out of bed because it was so comfortable. The views from my veranda stretched out over what seemed the whole of Damaraland.

As I was wolfing down my breakfast in anticipation of a quick departure, I overheard Bons talking to the trackers via radio, who were already out on the ground. The trackers were a dedicated team of four who dealt with this section of the concession and, although the rhinos were known individually, they still had to track them just using their incredible skills. The rhinos were not radio-collared, had vast territories, and were easily spooked. Bons and I had to be ready to spring into action once the location of a rhino had been determined. The only issue was that the trackers were about two hours away, so we had to get a wriggle on.

"Have you left the camp yet?" asked the voice on the other end of the radio.

"Just leaving now," said Bons as I stuffed a muffin in my mouth and gulped down the last of my tea.

What an adventure this is going to be, I thought.

We left promptly after that and drove for two hours through the undulating terrain of Damaraland. It is difficult to do justice in describing the scenery, it just blew my mind. If you are into panoramic views and contrasting colours; are at one with nature; marvelling at the ever-changing views; enjoy the anticipation of what is over the next horizon; and love standing in the middle of nowhere knowing that you are the only people for miles around, then this is certainly the place for you. I absolutely revelled in the place.

The radio sparked into life. They had spotted a rhino and her calf and if we got there quickly we would be able to see them. Bons floored the Land Rover and we bounced along the track. Then we came to an abrupt stop. I did a 360, looking around, I couldn't see any rhino... or any trackers for that matter.

"We will walk from here," said Bons, as he quickly got out of the Land Rover and hastily threw a few things into a small backpack; drinks, snacks, first aid kit, and a radio. I followed suit, put my day sack on, made sure I was smothered in sun cream, checked that I had my hat and sunglasses, and, most important of all, my camera. Then we walked into the middle of nowhere. It felt natural to me and the sense of being at peace as we walked away from the Land Rover was extraordinary. Once I couldn't see the Land Rover any longer I had the most amazing feeling of freedom.

Eventually, on the horizon, I spotted the two trackers standing on a small escarpment looking into a riverbed. After more walking we joined them.

They said they were waiting for the vehicle, as it had their camera in it. One of the jobs of the trackers is to take notes of every rhino sighted; rough age, distinguishing features on its ears, location, and another is to take pictures. These two had been walking for miles and miles, tracking the rhinos, and they had to wait for the vehicle to catch up as they hadn't got their camera with them. What surprised me most was that they had no water or food – nothing. I don't know how they survived. I'd already drunk half a litre just walking from the vehicle. The pressing issue was the lack of the rhino camera.

"I have a camera, would that help?" I offered. It did help. We worked out how we could download the photos, and made a plan. The plan was this: I was not to get charged by a rhino. I liked the plan.

I was given strict instructions to stay with Bons at all times, even if the trackers moved away from us. If a rhino did make any sudden movements, or looked like it was in charging mode, the trackers would draw it away from me, keeping me safe. I was a bit concerned about this. What about everyone else? Why should I take precedence? Having said that, I certainly wasn't going to argue with the wealth of expertise that was standing around me. Wild animals can be unpredictable, yet these men would be able to read them much better than I ever could.

Heart-in-mouth (mine not theirs), we moved into the river bed and lying there, were two rhinos, mother and calf.

We circumnavigated them as quietly as possible, so that we could approach from a different angle with plenty of cover. I was conscious of my new job as official photographer, so I had my camera at the ready. I did my best to tread quietly and to match my steps with Bons.

We walked within 50m, then 40m, and at 30m my heart was racing, (so loud I was sure that even the rhinos would be able to hear me). Bons gestured to me to move forward and to take my photos.

Click.

Ears twitched.

Click.

She got up.

Click.

The youngster also got up and the mother snorted.

The problem with DSLR cameras is that they do make a little bit of noise. Unfortunately, I had spooked both rhinos and they were now aware of us, although they couldn't see us. I raised my head above the parapet of the rocky outcrop and ran off a few more shots, encouraged enthusiastically by both the trackers and Bons to take as many as possible. They needed the photos for crucial identification. It was then that the rhinos took off into the wilderness, I was amazed at how fast they moved.

I suspect that some people might be disappointed about the skittishness of the rhinos, but I'm pleased that they are twitchy and have not become habituated to the presence of humans. This bodes well for their future, especially when they are in the safe hands of *Save The Rhino Trust*.

That evening I downloaded my photos onto the Trust's computer. Everyone was pleased with the photos that I had taken. I had done my small part in conserving these rhinos, albeit a very, very small one.

Buffalo Ambush

While I was working in Zimbabwe, I had the opportunity to visit Bumi Hills, a fantastic lodge up on the edge of Lake Kariba with views to die for. I was working in *Save Valley Conservancy* and I was sponsored by Zimbabwe Sun Hotels. It was a great opportunity as I got to visit a lot of the top hotels in Zimbabwe and stay for free. That was only if I was going with one of the ZimSun hotel representatives. I couldn't just march into a hotel and expect free board and lodging.

There I was, in a small plane, being flown up to Bumi Hills for the day. After a few buzzes over the airstrip, to encourage the resident giraffes to move off the landing strip, we safely landed on the shores of Lake Kariba.

We drove to the lodge and I was shown to my room. Firstly, I was not expecting my own room; I thought that I was there for a day, (although I had been warned to pack for a few days just in case we had to stay overnight or longer). Secondly, the room was set in a stunning location that left my mouth wide open. The room was on the top of an escarpment overlooking Lake Kariba. It was so high up that I could see the back of a bateleur eagle flying below, the balcony being suspended out over the dizzy heights of Kariba plains. Everything had been thought of with the architecture blending into the natural surroundings.

It was also siesta time so, in true African style, I had an hour-long snooze and then got up to look for the others to see what was happening.

I was hoping that there was a chance of a game drive before leaving. I was in time for a drive, but the rest had left me behind, and said that they would pick me up in five days' time. What a lovely surprise! Although knowing about it might have been easier for me to manage, but the thought did count! I was to stay longer than I'd hoped for, to learn more about the wildlife and to increase my general knowledge about all things African. I was amazed, what an opportunity to be given, and how generous. I embraced it with both arms.

So began my extravaganza of learning from the guides, and going out with them to do survey work, check on the wildlife, and generally be part of the crew. There were no clients here so I mucked in with them as a member of staff.

I went bug collecting, tree sampling, and dung analysing. I learnt about butterflies, the resident elephants, and how to track buffalos. The tracking and what to do came in handy the following day; it was a good job that I had been paying attention.

I was out with one of the guides and we went to check on the whereabouts of the local herd of buffalo and some other wildlife that needed locating. It was more of a a jolly whilst walking in the bush but with the premise that we were doing a bit of work.

Buffalo are one of the Big Five – dangerous animals not to be messed with, and worthy of respect. There are two types of herd that are normally found in Africa. First are the main breeding herds with a dominant male, females, and calves. Second are the smaller bachelor herds comprising young males (that re-join the breeding herd as they get older), and older males (that remain outside the herd as they can no longer compete with younger bulls). The older males are often called 'dagga boys' as they spend most of their time wallowing in dagga, (Zulu for *mud*), which helps to prevent flies landing on them. The dagga boys are no longer strong enough to compete for breeding rights and are therefore rather hacked off with life, taking their anger out on most things. They are best avoided at all costs.

It was these boys that we accidentally stumbled upon. We had been watching the main herd and were walking back to the lodge when we realised that we had just entered a group of dagga boys. The tell-tale snap of a twig alerted us, but that was all the warning we got and they knew we were there too. I immediately put a tree between me and the buffalo, it was a rather thin tree, but any tree, whatever its size, was better than no tree at all. Well, it felt better for me anyway.

I held my breath. No large crashing came through the undergrowth, no sudden movements, no bellowing – we were safe for the moment.

There were eight that I could see nearby, but I was certain that there were others in the bushes further away from us, I could hear them feeding in the dense bush. I checked all around me and ensured that my tree was in the right place in relation to the buffalo. There was none behind us, which was a good thing. I did not want a buffalo to sneak up on me, which they can do. My hearing was on high alert.

The next issue was how we were going to extract ourselves from the situation. Quietly was the best option and preferably with limbs intact. I felt like I was in a Tom and Jerry cartoon, as we tippy-toed from one thin tree to the next, trying to make ourselves slim to hide behind each tree. I could even hear the piano-tinkle noise of my own cartoon soundtrack in my head as we moved from one hiding place to the next, and felt my heart exploding out of my chest. If it had not been so scary it would have been funny. I am certain that I now hold the world record for the longest held breath, it felt like half an hour.

Eventually, we emerged out of our buffalo ambush, unscathed and relieved. With a tentative scanning of the area we made it to the bar for a beer. Trust me, a beer has never tasted so good.

Even now, after all these years of being in the

bush, buffalo make me twitchy when I am on foot.

The sounds of the African bush are incredible to experience, although it is always handy to know what is actually making the noise. Even if this does scare you more, knowledge is power.

Houseboat Bliss

I had no expectations for my stay on a houseboat, I had no idea what I was letting myself in for. What a fabulous surprise it turned out to be.

I was met by Luke from the houseboat, *The Pride of the Zambezi*, and he accompanied me through the Botswanan border control and I officially left the country. I was then taken by a small power boat for a ten-minute journey across the Chobe River to Namibia on the other side.

The border post here was even more remote than the one in Botswana. To begin with I couldn't even find the man to stamp my passport for me – he was having a snooze around the back. I think that day I had been his second visitor, so not an overly stressful job. In fact, it was more traumatic for me trying to find him, and I was meant to be on holiday!

All houseboats are registered in Namibia because they allow fishing on the River Chobe, whereas Botswana does not. Fishing is one of the more popular activities on houseboats, although if you're into wildlife photography then it does not matter where the boat is registered.

Luke and I then set off in the boat to find my bedroom for the next two nights. The houseboat was about thirty minutes west up the River Chobe. The journey was a speedboat ride and I felt as if I was in a wind tunnel for half an hour, it was exhilarating. We carved round enormous pods of hippos, spotted herds of elephants on the riverbank, sped past regal fish eagles as they perched precariously on tree branches above our heads, and gave a wide berth to skittish impala drinking at the water's edge. I put on my sunglasses, sipped my beer and enjoyed the ride.

Then we arrived at my home for the next two days, floating idly with the current, nestling amongst waterlilies. I was enthusiastically welcomed aboard and given a quick guided tour around the boat.

The setup is incredible. There are four cabins downstairs, all of which are ensuite and every room has enormous windows looking out over the water. I kept my curtains open during the night so that the twinkling stars could keep me company.

The main deck area is a large, open plan room with a bar, a large table for supper, and comfy couches. There were decked areas at the front and the back of the boat, and even a jacuzzi! The top deck is where the captain pilots our mobile home, along with a luxury cabin with private decking and another spacious room. After my tour, I got back to the main decking area to find lunch been laid out on a little table facing out over the Chobe River, absolute bliss.

You settle into the routine of a houseboat far too easily. Each cabin has its own small boat so that occupants can go fishing whenever they feel like it, or take their own self-guided game-viewing tour.

There is also a larger boat that can seat all ten

guests, and this was ideal for going for sunrise and sundowner cruises. During the day, the houseboat would chug leisurely up and down the Chobe River in search of interesting animals or good fishing spots.

This particular houseboat is one of the few that has permission to moor up within Chobe National Park, meaning that at the end of the evening and at the beginning of the day you have the whole of the river frontage to yourself. Only a couple of other boats are on the river, and all the safari vehicles have to be out of the park. It is a real pleasure to experience the peace and tranquillity of the park, that is apart from the regular, raucous honking of hippos, which is, of course, perfectly acceptable.

That evening, I went out on a sundowner boat cruise and as I sipped my gin and tonic I saw elephants drinking from the water's edge, only 10m away, a huge flock of bee-eaters chitter-chattering to each other as they dove in and out of their mud nests, and a troop of baboons causing mischief with a lone impala. But there was more to come. As we had our three-course dinner we heard lions roaring nearby. We just about heard them over the clink of glasses and the appreciative sounds of people eating delicious steaks.

SMELL

Africa has a distinctive smell, just like any other continent. I often associate the smell of the African bush with hard-baked earth; the pungent aroma of wildlife; and the dry, crispness of the vegetation. Mix them all together and that is the African savannah for you.

The earth is so dry and every ounce of moisture is sucked out by the sun, water does not stand a chance. Water has a distinctive smell, whether it be a small river or a waterhole. Initially, it smells sweet and fresh but the drier the terrain gets, just before the rains, the more acrid-smelling the mud surrounding waterholes becomes as wildlife visit the diminishing resource.

However, one of the best smells is that of a braai, the smell of chicken and steak sizzling on the fire, the burning wood and the ice-cold beer in your hand - simply perfect.

Bush Toilets

I often get asked about what it is like going to the loo in Africa. Normally, it is fine. Quite often there are flushing toilets, running water and all the mod cons that you probably take for granted. However, in the remote bush camps there is often no electricity, so a head torch is often a good piece of kit to have. Normally though, the loos are not that different to the ones we are used to.

I have used some spectacular 'thrones' in my time in Africa. There's nothing quite like looking out into the bush whilst doing your business, and once I saw a rhino walk by. I can honestly say that I spent longer in that particular loo!

In the up-market lodges the toilets can be pristine and overtly luxurious. The bush camp experience can be surprising, and in a pleasant way. Candles light up the pathway leading to your toilet, quirky extras such as a chain to put across the entrance to let others know that it is in use, and some are so spacious that they are larger than the footprint of my flat.

Bush toilets are normally in stunning settings. The best one I have used was overlooking the Zambezi River and whilst I was there I watched a herd of elephants sploshing around in the water. That certainly was a loo with a view.

In the more remote and adventurous locations there are a variety of different kinds of loos termed long drops, which become short drops as more people use them. Some are more unpleasant than others, so make sure that you use one that looks solid in structure. The thought of everything crashing in around you may make your visit to the loo shorter!

I have been in a rural long drop where I nearly lost my balance on the precarious logs that I was supposed to stand on. I grabbed hold of the flimsy wall, and proceeded to dismantle the structure surrounding me. Luckily, I managed to remain decent and upstanding, which is more than the former toilet did.

It was rather embarrassing and I helped to reassemble the toilet walls, surrounded by a lot of angry, buzzing flies. It was not one of my more graceful moments in life.

There's a long drop in Hlane, Swaziland, that can be traumatic for those who go in the middle of the night. It's in a bush camp in a remote part of the park so it's not used often. Well, it is used, but not for its intended purpose. A colony of bats have taken up residence, which can be disconcerting when trying to have a wee in the middle of the night. I found that the best thing to do is to shine a torch across the hole of the toilet to encourage the bats to fly out before using the loo. Once you know this trick it isn't much of an issue, but for those that don't it can be a surprising experience. Bats bashing your bottom is not a pleasant feeling.

There are some loos that are even less desirable and sometimes I cannot believe what I am seeing and wonder whether common sense was not packed when leaving the UK.

I was working with volunteers in the south east lowveld of Zimbabwe. We were all staying in a remote bush camp in *Save Valley Conservancy* where there was a large long drop that had been there for a number of years. I say large, it was about 10m deep, 8m wide, and had the potential to be there for another few years. The whole structure looked as if it had been built over a termite mound, which maybe it had, so the excavation of it might well have been a bit easier. It looked structurally sound and the tree trunks across the hole and supporting the loo were still solid. No chance of the whole lot collapsing whilst sitting there minding your own business - my worst nightmare.

There were fifteen of us in the camp at the time and I was permanently based there: managing the scientific work of analysing the grass biomass in the area; tracking black rhino with rangers and GPS for the dehorning team to come in; and monitoring pit fall traps to log the small mammals and reptiles that frequented the area.

It was normally a noisy camp with lots of things happening, but as I emerged from my mud hut (I was living in a mud hut for ten weeks at a time) it was abnormally quiet. This made me twitchy. I could hear some hushed voices coming from the long drop area so I went to investigate. After all, I was responsible for everyone's welfare. And there, was the most ridiculous, unbelievable, heart-stopping vision in front of me – two guys holding the feet of a third person suspended head down inside the long drop. I could only see his knees and feet protruding from the toilet seat.

The previous night, Dan had dropped his head torch into the long drop while it was turned on, and it lit up the inside of the cavern like a beacon, projecting a beam into the night sky akin to Batman's distress signal. Going to the loo after that had been a bit disconcerting as you could see (if you chose to look) the large albino python that lived in the depths, and the numerous bats that it fed off. The light had flustered the bats and they were active all night, and all day as well. Going to the loo became an interesting challenge. It had been decided to leave the torch where it was, and let the batteries run down – I thought that this was sensible, and the only option.

Obviously, Dan thought differently, and had decided that he wanted his torch back as he didn't have another one. There he was, suspended over a soup of human and bat faeces, reaching down to retrieve his torch. The smell alone must have made him gag. I was aghast. What on earth was he thinking? I did wonder whether he would want to wear his head torch after knowing where it had been, the health implications were disgusting.

"Please pull Dan out of there immediately," I said in a calm and commanding voice. At least that is what I thought I sounded like, it was probably more of a squeak.

Inside I was in utter turmoil. If he had fallen he would have probably died from either drowning, asphyxiation, the crush from a hacked-off snake, or from any one of a host of diseases such as typhoid, cholera, hepatitis A, tetanus, dysentery... the list was endless. I had no idea how I was going to explain that.

Slowly, Dan was extracted from the long drop, inch by inch, and there was a collective sigh of relief from all the spectators when his feet were firmly placed on the ground. He looked relieved, and out of breath. I advised him that it might be a good idea to have a shower in disinfectant, to take a few deep breaths of fresh air, and to contemplate his stupidity.

That night, and the next, the bats and python had to endure the illumination, as did those going to the loo – they were exceptionally good batteries.

Endure Nasal Assaults for Incredible Sightings

When travelling to Namibia you never expect seals to be on your safari list. Namibia is famous for Etosha and its wide-open spaces with shimmering herds of springbok, but seals are never top of the 'must see' safari animals. However, the seal colony at Cape Cross, approximately 130km north of Swakopmund, should not to be missed and will certainly be something that your olfactory glands will remember.

The colony is easily accessed from the main road running north up the Skeleton Coast and as I drove along the bumpy road I marvelled at the raw and inhospitable coastline. Nothing seemed to be growing here and the waves were relentlessly crashing onto the unforgiving shore. As I was wondering how long I was going to drive along this road, and whether I was going in the right direction, there appeared to be what I could only presume was a car park. The reason why I thought it was a car park was because there was a small brick wall preventing any further adventurous travel. I had arrived.

The Cape Cross Seal Reserve was created in 1968 to protect the largest and best-known Cape fur seal colony along the Namibian coast. Fur seals are commonly known as brown seals, and are more closely related to sea lions than to true seals. They share external ears, relatively long and muscular fore-flippers, and the ability to walk on all fours. True seals are sometimes called crawling seals and do not possess external ears.

The amazing thing is that this reserve is the largest mainland breeding colony of Cape Fur Seals in Namibia, numbering between 80,000 and 100,000. It is an incredible sight to behold.

On the other side of the wall was a sea of seals. It was a gobsmacking sight. I still had my mouth open as I opened the car door, and the stench of the seals was completely overwhelming, making me gag. There was no way you could escape the smell, a hand over your nose and mouth only slightly diminished the impact and breathing through your mouth had no effect at all, it was incredible. The smell was of hot, wet, damp, unwashed, seal bodies blended with the acrid stench of seal dung that had spent too much time in the Namibian sun. It was completely overpowering and now I understood why I had been recommended to make only a short visit.

With the smell came the noise, a cacophony of mother seals calling for their pups, lost pups mewing for their mothers, and aggressive interactions occurring all over the limited rock space. It was an assault on my senses.

I was particularly careful not to make any sudden movements and definitely not to approach too closely. It has been known for the seals to get spooked and as a result pups get trampled to death. The seals seemed unperturbed and I had a wonderful half hour of seal-watching before the foul stench and incessant noise drove me bonkers.

Getting into my car provided a happy respite for my ears, but a minimal amount of nasal relief and only by driving a considerable distance away from the colony could I allow my nose to recover from its horrific ordeal.

Seeing incredible things in Africa sometimes comes at a price! I remember seeing three of the Big Five, (elephant, rhino, and buffalo), in a mud wallow, one after another, but again my nose had to suffer to get the most out of it.

There was mud flying everywhere, high into the trees, out of the wallow, and over everything in sight. Glorious, glorious, mud. The elephants were having a magnificent time and this was apparent by the low rumblings of the older elephants and the odd excited squeal from the younger ones.

And the smell! The smell carried on the gentle breeze to us, so we could really appreciate the experience. I have to say the smell of the thick, gloopy mud had a hint of vegetation and a copious amount of dung. The smell was further heightened by the heat of the day to create an eye-watering sewage experience on our nasal cavities. It invaded our senses and I felt as if I could actually taste the mud in the back of my mouth. It also felt as if I was wearing a sheen of dung over my body, the smell was so strong.

We were on Safari in Mkhaya Game Reserve in the Kingdom of Swaziland and within thirty minutes of our first game drive we found these elephants having a wonderful time in the middle of the day. Some of the elephants ventured into the middle of the mud wallow and we could hear the suction noises as they pulled their feet out of the gloopy mess. Others were more contented staying on the periphery and expertly throwing mud over their backs to cool off from the heat of the day. And with every throw of mud came a waft of raw Africa.

I was concerned. I didn't want to be covered in filth right at the beginning of the game drive and we were rather close to the mud wallow.

Wallowing acts as a cooling method. Warthogs and buffalos spend time lying in mud-wallows to reduce their body temperature. Rhinos will cover their bodies in mud for the same reason, and then retreat to a shady area out of the sun. Elephants love the cooling effect of mud to regulate their body temperature and will often submerge themselves in water before their mud or sand bath.

For all these species, the mud also acts as protection against sunburn and provides relief from biting insects. A wallow in a muddy puddle is normally followed by a good scratch against a strong rubbing post. This removes ticks and other skin parasites that become embedded in the mud. A rubbing post can be a tree, a rock, or a termite mound. Much-used rubbing posts can eventually become smooth and shiny and are easy to identify.

The elephants were the first of the Big Five to visit this wallow. The second was approaching to the left, weaving their way through the foliage and making a beeline for the cooling mud. Four white rhinos were measured up by the herd of elephants. The rhinos squared up to the elephants, and a stand-off ensued. It was one of those questions that people often ask, "Who would win in a fight between an elephant and a white rhino?"

In this case, the rhino won.

Or maybe the elephants let them win as they

made it look as if they were leaving anyway. The elephants nonchalantly moved away from the mud wallow, I suspected they had had their fill. Which still begs the question as to who would win between an elephant and a white rhino in a fight.

The four rhinos practically leapt into the wallow and you could feel their contentment as they nestled and nuzzled their way into the cooling mud, the ultimate bed. It was relaxing to watch. Any movement from the rhinos sent more sewage scent towards us.

Then the third of the Big Five arrived at the mud wallow, three old dagga boys – old male buffalo. The buffalo surveyed the area, weighing up their chances of gaining access to the mud. The rhinos didn't even acknowledge their presence. The buffalo walked around the mud wallow, inspecting it from all angles, and realised that this time the wallow was not theirs. They sauntered off into the bush in search of a more accessible mud bath.

It was an extraordinary scene that we had just witnessed, heard, and smelled. Note to self: next time bring some nasal plugs.

Rain, I can Smell it Coming

I arrived in Zimbabwe in July 1992, in the midst of a drought that the country had not seen for decades. The rains in December 1991 had not materialised, and there had not been any decent rain on the hard-baked, thirsty land for over a year. Not only were the animals starving, but also the people.

I remember driving down from Harare *to Save Valley Conservancy* and seeing miles upon miles of failing maize, withered tobacco plants, bare vegetable plots, and mostly deserted villages. There was nothing to celebrate, no food on plates, and the people that I did see were sitting listlessly in the shade by the side of the road.

When I first journeyed through *Save Valley Conservancy* to Devuli Ranch where I was to live, the impact of the drought on the wildlife also hit me hard. Herds of impala made up of skin and bones sheltered under wizened trees, the flies buzzing around them and only a shake of the head or a quick flick of the tail could remove these pests, albeit only for a second.

The first impala that I saw close-up died in front of my vehicle. It wasn't because I'd hit it; this particular impala no longer had the energy to continue walking and it just so happened that it collapsed in front of me. I believe that my approach probably caused its demise due to fright, on top of dehydration and starvation. If I'd had any sense I would have put the carcass in the back of my vehicle and handed it into the rangers but I left it where it lay, and the circling vultures probably had another feast that day. At least some animals were benefiting from the drought.

Over the coming months, I spent a lot of time out in the bush and there was one sense that assailed me practically every single day – the stench of death. It was an overpowering, pungent smell and my sense of smell became so in tune with the sickly stench that I could soon discern how long ago the animal had died before approaching it. As time passed, it became such a common smell that I learned to block it out, only registering the fact that an animal had died. The aroma no longer made me gag, and I became hardened to it.

To begin with, finding animal carcasses had been tremendously upsetting but, after living with it for many months, it simply became a part of life. Life and death are very much in your face in the bush. Death was there, lingering, waiting, clapping its hands with glee, and laughing at its own good luck.

I survived the suicide month of October, so-called because the heat and humidity can become unbearable, and this is the time when more people take their own lives as they cannot cope with the high temperatures, lack of sleep, dehydration, and the financial loss of failed crops.

Every day I had to dry my sweat-sodden mattress in the sun, before going through the torturous business of getting some sleep the following night. I endured the nights by putting some water into my bath, so every time I woke up in a pool of sweat I could splash myself in the water and then stagger back to my bed slightly cooler for a short while. I would then pray that I would get another couple of hours of sleep before waking up again, but if this did not happen it was a trip back to the bath to go through the same process again. I also had to fish out bugs and any hapless animals that had found their way into my cooling system. My bath had the same brackish water for three weeks; clean water every day was too much of a luxury.

I was beginning to become immune to the sight of suffering due to drought in the conservancy area. The impala and wildebeest no longer looked like bags of bones to me, the lack of leaves on the normally green mopane trees became the usual part of my bush experience, and the parched, dry, crazy-paved pans devoid of water were accepted in my mind as normal. It was only much later that I fully appreciated how unhealthy the wildlife had been. Even today, when I see a perfectly healthy impala grazing, in my mind I am thinking *My God, that impala is fat!*

The rains were late again. Zimbabwe normally experiences some rain in October or November, and halfway into December there was still no sign of the much-needed water. People were nervous and many livelihoods were now at stake due to the lack of rain. Tempers were frayed and money was being lost like dry sand dribbling through fingers. When were we going to get some respite from it all?

Christmas of 1992 was a memorable affair. Despite the lack of rain, we all went about our Christmas celebrations as per usual. Derek and Margaret, the owners of Devuli Ranch, had invited their family over to stay and I had a whole load of guests in my house as well. People were travelling from miles around to come and stay and Christmas Eve was the day of travel.

Devuli Ranch is situated in the northern section of *Save Valley Conservancy*, and there are two dry riverbeds to cross to get to the ranch. These had obviously been dry for many months and the compacted sand was easy to drive across, even in a two-wheel-drive vehicle. Access to Devuli had been ridiculously easy for a while.

It was around lunchtime that I noticed the change. I noticed that things were different, and it took a while for me to recognise what they were.

It was the smell; the very smell of the country had changed. It no longer smelled of dry dust, of hard-baked soil, of the smell that I had become accustomed to. There was an earthier smell now, it was neither a more pleasant nor unpleasant smell, but was just different. As the minutes ticked on, this smell became sweeter and gave with it a sense of hope. What I was smelling was the smell of the coming rain.

A breeze began to stir on the otherwise lifeless ground and the smell of rain became deeper. I have never experienced anything like this before. I think I could smell the rain when it was still over 200km away. For over three hours we waited for this life-giving rain. It seemed as if we were all waiting, the animals looked expectant, people had a sense of nervous energy, yet we knew we must wait just that little bit longer for the anticipated miracle.

The smell became stronger and stronger. It became addictive and I couldn't stay inside. I had to stand outside and just sniff the air, registering the different smells that were carried on the cool breeze; damp tarmac, wet earth, fresh vegetation, it was all there. The sense of urgency became greater and I found myself getting twitchy, expectantly waiting for the restoration of life.

The rain hit at around five o'clock in the afternoon, and it was torrential. To begin with there was a sudden rush of wind, sending dry leaves, dust, twigs and any other flotsam of the bush into the air, swirling around haphazardly, as a warning bell for the coming downpour.

The aroma of warm, sodden earth was so strong it was intoxicating. And as the rain fell it was such a glorious feeling that I remember laughing out loud. I think my guests must have thought that I had become possessed as I ran around outside, arms outstretched, dancing in the rain. I was not the only one out in the elements, Derek and Margaret were there too, champagne glasses in hand, celebrating the arrival of the rain. My guests had not been in Africa long and understandably could not comprehend its significance and how relieved we all were, but I will never forget standing in the rain with Derek and Margaret, toasting the heavens.

I don't think I've ever seen so much rain fall in so little time, and that is in all my time in Africa. Derek and Margaret's family got caught in the rain and the dry riverbed crossings became a torrential mass of churning liquid chocolate filled with debris – branches, whole trees, sheets of corrugated iron, and goodness knows what else. The causeway and dry river crossing had been swept away, making it completely impassable and it trapped their family on an island surrounded by angry water, only 200m from the house. No 4x4 vehicle was going to drive through this flood, but everyone was happy to wait. We had waited over a year for rains, another twelve hours was nothing in the grand scheme of things.

We spent an hour on the riverbank, shouting across different messages and dancing back and forth before retiring to bed. Derek and Margaret's family hunkered down to a rather uncomfortable night in their cars. The smell of rain in Africa is a wonderful experience, it seems to cleanse the environment as well as your soul.

The Lioness nearly ate my Bacon

Mana Pools, in Zimbabwe, is an extraordinary place and I would certainly classify it as one of the true wildernesses of Africa. I suppose that I have a great affinity for this place as this was my first experience in an African game reserve, other than *Save Valley Conservancy*, which is where I was working at the time. *Save Valley Conservancy* is a group of 19 landowners who came together to form a vast tract of land for wild animals. When I was there it was in its infancy, changing over from cattle to game and becoming dedicated to the conservation of wildlife and their habitats. It was going to be a long process. I was delighted to be visiting a game reserve where it was wildlife all the way, and a haven for the Big Five.

Mana Pools is a wildlife conservation area in northern Zimbabwe on the banks of the River Zambezi that has been designated as a UNESCO World Heritage Site. It is the region on the lower Zambezi where the flood plains turn into a broad expanse of lakes after the rainy season. As the lakes gradually dry up and recede, the region attracts many large animals in search of water, making it one of Africa's most renowned game regions.

'Mana' means 'four' in Shona, which refers to the four permanent pools formed by the meanderings of the river. The 2,500 km^2 of river frontage, islands, sandbanks, and pools, flanked by forests of mahogany, wild figs, ebonies, and baobabs, is one of the least-developed national parks in southern Africa. Words can't fully describe how stunning the area is.

Accompanying the incredible scenery are huge herds of elephants, buffalos, zebras, waterbucks, and many other species of antelope. Of course, that means their associated predators including lions and hyenas also migrate to the area each year during the dry winter months. The river is also famous for its sizeable numbers of hippopotamuses and Nile crocodiles.

I was fortunate to be camping in one of the remote campsites of Mana Pools. In fact, it was the camp furthest from the main tourism area. In the early 1990s, there was little infrastructure supporting Mana Pools, you were left to your own devices. In order to use these wilderness camps you had to have a registered hunter with a firearms licence in the group. You really are stuck out in the middle of a wilderness amongst the wildlife of Africa, and safety is paramount. One of our group, Stewart, was a professional guide so he was permitted to carry his firearm into the reserve. It was a big thing for me to be remote camping in Mana Pools, something that I hadn't fully appreciated until a bit later in our trip.

We had a wonderful campsite on a small, raised mound, overlooking the River Zambezi, with the most incredible vista along the floodplains and across the river. The only structure to indicate that we were at a campsite at all was the concrete braai that had obviously been used as a rubbing post by a passing elephant or two. It looked a bit tired and was standing at a rather jaunty angle and the grill was warped. Despite all of this it was still functional, which was a good thing as we cooked all our meals on it. Behind us were a few trees dotted around the bushveld where herds of elephants roamed.

That evening we sat on our raised mound with the braai crackling in the background and the strong aroma of sausages, onions, and steak gently wafting around us. The smell was saliva-inducing and I wished that the sausages would hurry up and cook. To keep our minds off the food we watched a vast herd of elephants lumber gracefully down to the river to drink. To the left of us was a herd of impala, skittishly browsing and wary of predators. Night was drawing in and monkeys chitter-chattered from the trees hanging over the campsite drawn to the smell of our delicious food. Small, colourful birds flitted from one branch to another. It was enchanting.

Just as the sun was setting, and the sausages were nearly edible, up padded a pride of lions into the twilight to drink at the river's edge. I could make out the large male lion and lionesses and their cubs. I counted at least nine in the group, although I suspected that there were a few stealthy ones elsewhere, invisible in the shadows of the trees. We all squinted, trying to see the pride, but they had come to drink under the cover of darkness. No wonder the impala had a heightened nervousness about them.

The sun set over the bushveld and, after eating under a star pricked sky – food always tastes better when cooked and eaten outside – we crawled contentedly into our tents. Then the excitement began.

During the night there was a lot of lion activity down on the floodplains: roaring throughout the night; clashes between nervous lionesses trying to prevent a takeover; and mewing of cubs caught in the fracas. It was apparent that a younger lion was challenging the older lion for control of the pride, and it sounded as if he was winning. It was surprising if anyone got any sleep at all – I certainly didn't. Unfortunately, we had no opportunity to see what was taking place.

In the morning, I tentatively got out of my tent to find Stewart, who, gun in hand, was standing on the outskirts of our campsite checking the area. The larger lion was still defending his pride from the younger male; they were circling each other displaying their strength and strutting backwards and forwards, manes puffed up and looking tremendous. The lionesses had scattered into small groups, ears flattened, awaiting the outcome. All of this was taking place just 200m from our campsite.

I started the braai for our breakfast of bacon and eggs, while Stewart kept an eye on our neighbours. The two males were having a stand-off, watching each other and planning their next move. The bacon was on the braai, sizzling away, smelling delicious, and the eggs were boiling – perfect. There were five of us in the group and we all stood cleaning our teeth, like sentinels, watching the lion saga unfold before us. It was like a BBC wildlife documentary, except it was full-screen.

"If any of those lionesses break away from the pride, get into the vehicle immediately," said Stewart, "Do not think about it, just do it." We all nodded, completely understanding the implications if we didn't act quickly.

Of course, this is what happened next; two lionesses broke away from the pride, coming in our direction at a steady trot, and we clambered over each other as we dived in through the windows of the car to get to safety. It did not take the lionesses long to cover the distance and within a minute they were in our campsite.

Unbeknown to us, there was another lioness in the area with her two young cubs and she was protecting them from being trampled in the heated fight. She was in the bushes behind the campsite, protecting her cubs from the new male. Killing her cubs would bring her back into breeding condition, so she could mate with the new male and give birth to his cubs. There would be no point for the new male in nurturing the cubs of another male. The lioness and her cubs were not an immediate threat to us, as they were keeping their distance from the newcomer, but it was still a hairy experience having these five visitors in our camp.

They smelled the bacon... inching closer to *my* breakfast, checking out what the mouth-watering smell was. To my mind this was not acceptable behaviour. There was no way I was going to let my breakfast be consumed by those cats. That was not an option.

As I happened to be sitting in the driver's seat I decided to take direct action. With some careful manoeuvring, backwards and forwards Austin Powers style, I managed to position our vehicle right next to the braai so that I could safely finish cooking breakfast through the open window. The car would also deter the lions from coming any closer to our scrumptious-smelling food. Stewart, meanwhile, kept a diligent lookout for our visitors, letting me know when it was safe to reach out of the car.

On Stewart's command, I reached for the rolls and smothered them in butter, turned the bacon, added them to the rolls, retrieved the eggs, drained them, peeled them, added tomato sauce, and handed breakfast-in-a-bun to the guys in the back via the outside windows. It was a rather long and drawn-out process as Stuart kept interrupting my duties with a variety of commands including "Stop!", "Carry on", "Get your arms in!", "Wait, she is just behind us", "Wind the window up, NOW!" and "Hurry up Jenny, I'm hungry."

That is my memory of Mana Pools; the glorious smell of bacon and eggs cooked on a braai, dispensing it as if I was in a Drive Thru, while surrounded by salivating lions.

TASTE

The taste of a whole fillet steak that has just come off the braai, sliced to show the pink inside and when you pick it up it slightly burns your fingers, probably sums up the taste of Africa for me, my mouth is watering as I write these words. Whether it be garlic prawns sizzling on the braai or butternut squash with feta gently melting through, there is something special about dining out under the stars at night, around a campfire, with the sounds of the bush as your own personal symphony.

On the flipside, there are some horrendous things that I have eaten in Africa, seen other people eat, and also have been offered and had the opportunity to decline politely. These 'delights' are more akin to the bush tucker trials than anything healthy. Thinking about these makes my mouth begin to salivate in preparation for me being sick and I dry heave.

However, there is always something delicious and tasty on offer, but it's sprinkled with a dash of advice of what *not* to eat!

Worms and Walkie-Talkies

Here are my top three worst dishes that I have eaten whilst overseas; third place goes to a goat's head (brains and all), second place to a fruit bat, and first place to a mopane worm.

The mopane worm, which is in fact a caterpillar, was offered to me by an old, wizened lady that I met out in the bush. She kindly offered up her bowl of nutritious, boiled mopane worms. The students that I was with all recoiled in horror and took a step backwards when she offered us the dish. However, it now looked as if I had stepped forward. I didn't want to offend this lady. Somebody had to accept her kind and generous offering, so I reached into the pot.

I estimated that the worm was too large for me to swallow whole, so I had to bite it. Unfortunately, when I bit into it I did not bite through the whole worm, so when I pulled the half away its innards ended up dangling down my chin, bits of entrails, nervous system, and arteries hanging there attractively. The only way to save face was to slurp up the entrails like spaghetti, swallow quickly, pop the remaining half into my mouth and try not to gag in the process. I did the best I could by smiling at the lady and thanking her for the tasty morsel, while the rest of the group looked at me in horror, hands over their mouths.

Another revolting looking (and smelling) food is 'walkie-talkie', which is aptly named – the feet and heads of chickens. These are often sold in supermarkets in the fresh meat section along with intestines, lungs, and other sorts of offal. Normally they are neatly presented on a polystyrene tray with the feet and heads squashed together in an ugly mass. I have had the unfortunate misfortune to be stuck in the back of a truck with a woman who had a pot of boiled walkie-talkies. I endured an hour listening to her crunching her way through the gristly chicken feet and slurping the brains out of their heads. It made for revolting listening and the smell was stomach-churning. Luckily, I was not offered any this time.

The great thing about Africa is that there are so many delicious things on the menu. It caters for vegetarians, carnivores (that's me), people who eat inordinate amounts of fruit, healthy diets, and even junk food – which I do my best to avoid.

I often speak to guests who are concerned about what they're going to eat, they suspect that it might consist of the dreaded mopane worm or walkie-talkie. Not so. In fact, this is so far from the truth that it makes me laugh. I've only ever eaten mopane worms once, and once was enough. I love going to Africa because I know I'm going to eat healthy, tasty food. The food is fresh, (probably picked, dug up or killed that morning), generally untainted by additives and pesticides, and always tastes better when you eat it outside.

Fresh fruit and vegetables are available all year round, and they haven't been processed, injected, shaped, sprayed, packaged, moulded, battered, or conformed to a certain shape and size and then transported halfway across the world in a freezer container. Instead, they come as they are – malformed, distorted, bobbly, non-conformist, pure, and chemical-free. You can certainly taste the difference between a misshapen African tomato and a perfectly-formed, force-ripened one in the UK. The food is fresh from the ground, bush, or off the hoof. Marvellous,

A typical breakfast consists of fruit salad, yoghurt, freshly baked bread accompanied by the option of a cooked breakfast. The cooked breakfasts are divine – fresh eggs, boervors (beef sausages packed with nothing but meat and none of the other nasty stuff), bacon, and cooked tomato. What you might expect from a full English, but packed with so much more flavour.

Lunches are often on the move, a picnic spread on the bonnet of your safari vehicle consisting of salads, fresh meats, cold chicken, cheese and bread, maybe washed down with a cool, refreshing beer and ending with fruits like pawpaw, pineapple, bananas, or apples. This may also be accompanied by less healthy options of crisps, peanuts, and a chocolate bar.

The dinners in Africa are something to marvel at, sometimes half the animals you have seen that day are on the menu! Impala is a delicious meat, solid with little fat and tastes like venison. Kudu, nyala, and any of the other antelope are similar – each with its own distinctive gamey taste. Kudu curry is delicious and whenever it is on the menu I always choose it. Warthog is also a wonderful meat, again low in fat and exceptionally tasty, especially when cooked over an open fire. I would also suggest trying crocodile tail; it is a mixture between chicken and fish, solid and yet delicate in taste and texture. There are the more standard meats that we are accustomed to such as beef (the steaks are to die for), chicken, and pork.

Ostrich is also delicious, it is often served as

carpaccio and that comes highly recommended. Ostrich meat is considered healthy as it is low in fat and high in calcium, protein, and iron. Strangely, the meat from an ostrich comes from its legs, thighs, and back, it does not possess any breast meat. Some people say that it tastes a bit like beef, which I suppose it does, although it does have a chicken-like texture to it as well. In the south-east of Zimbabwe, ostrich farming became an additional income to assist farmers when their cattle farming land changed over to the wildlife reserve, *Save Valley Conservancy*.

One day I got roped into helping medicate them for ticks, ensuring they stayed healthy in their vast bush enclosure. I don't know what possessed me, but I stupidly agreed to help, not knowing what I was letting myself in for. Pre-requisites for this job include patience, eye-balling techniques, an ability to show no fear, and a good sense of humour, of which I possess only one attribute. Although, even my sense of humour temporarily vanished after ten minutes of scrabbling around in the dust.

Have you ever tried to catch an ostrich? Believe me, it's as hard as you think it is. First you must get within grabbing distance, which in itself isn't an easy feat, and then you then have to manoeuvre yourself into a safe position. This is because an ostrich has two toes on each foot, the first toe being exceptionally long and possessing a large toenail. A single swipe with that can disembowel a human. This little fact was prominent in my mind.

It is advisable to grab the ostrich by its neck and to swiftly force it down to the ground, this prevents it from gutting you as its head and neck are in the way of its vicious feet. Then, with syringe in hand, (that's if you have not dropped it whilst running around after said ostrich), the beak is prised open and the yellow medication is squirted into the bird's mouth.

At this point you might be mistaken in thinking that this is the end of your ordeal, but not so. There is now the tricky procedure of safely letting go of the ostrich's neck whilst performing a swift sidestep to avoid a big, angry, bird. Once released it is likely to swerve backwards and forwards, wings outstretched like battering rams. Then, it's on to the next one, heart in mouth.

That day I suffered a couple of knocks and one violent peck to my arm. I certainly will not be offering my services to the School of Ostrich Medication again. I'm much happier eating ostrich carpaccio than chasing the live animal around the bush. If you get the opportunity, do try ostrich, whether it is served as an appetiser or the main dish. Don't ask for a whole leg, as you might be there for a while!

Meat is an important part of the African diet but if you are a vegetarian then you are also in for a treat. Being a vegetarian in Africa can be easily catered for and there are certainly a host of wonderful, exotic, and intriguing things to eat.

Butternut is used a lot and when roasted and accompanied by feta cheese is absolutely delicious. There is also a wide selection of squashes of various shapes, sizes, and forms. Many have not reached UK shops, so try them all out, it is certainly worth it.

The avocados are the size of small rugby balls, oranges are exceptionally juicy, and pineapples are cut from the field that you passed twenty minutes earlier.

The list of vegetables and fruits available is practically never-ending; sweet potatoes, squash, cucumber, peppers, spinach, water lilies, salad onions, normal onions, all sorts of herbs, lychees, apricots, grapefruit, star fruit, pomegranates, carrots, oranges, courgettes, aubergine...

The whole experience of eating is helped by the atmosphere; dining on decking overlooking a watering hole with the sound of the bush in chorus around you and the big sky above, you cannot help being sucked into romantic notions as you dine. It is not just the dining experience that is memorable, it is also the knowledge that it will happen all over again tomorrow.

It is healthy eating with a healthy lifestyle. In fact, your whole system has a complete overhaul and, although you don't realise it, you are having a detox.

My advice would be to try everything. Be adventurous, eat something different, you might just love it. Mopane worms are optional.

Have Your Coke and Eat It

My brother, Jason, had never been to Africa before, so the obvious solution for him was to come with me. This was a few years back when I was working for a gap year organisation, setting up conservation and community projects in Swaziland. He came out with me on my recce for the next expedition, and we had a two-week holiday –a bit of a busman's holiday for me, but certainly a holiday for Jason.

We had some memorable experiences: a full day by Mahlindza Dam watching the animals come to drink; Jason spending a night snuggling up to some animal to keep warm in the night (whatever it was, it was on the other side of the tent and Jason had a good night's sleep); and the mist clearing to give the most spectacular view in Malolotja. One of the funniest situations we had was a lesson in communication.

We decided to have lunch in Simunye Country Club. There is a swimming pool there that we were taking advantage of as it was extraordinarily hot that day. Before taking a dip, we decided to have a drink, and Jason went to the bar to order. A few minutes later the waiter came out with my *Sprite* and disappeared back into the bar area. Jason's *Coke* wasn't there. I was halfway through my drink before Jason queried the fact that his was missing. It was a hot day and he was parched.

"Not to worry," I said, and I went over to the bar to find out where his drink was.

"I was just wondering where our *Coke* was," I asked.

"They're just making it now."

"They are just *making* it?"

"Yes, it will be ready in twenty minutes."

"A *Coke* takes twenty minutes to make?" I asked incredulously.

"Yes."

"Oh."

It then dawned on me what had happened. Jason had ordered a *Coke* but the waiter had misheard and thought he had said 'cake'. I felt terrible, the kitchen staff were slaving away over an unwanted cake.

"What type of cake are they making?"

"Plain."

"Please could we have two slices of plain cake and also a *Coca-Cola*?"

Well, we couldn't let the cake go to waste, could we? And it was worth every minute of the wait!

Eating a Goat's Head

I entered the darkened room and sat on the straw matting on the floor, I let my eyes adjust to the gloom – it took a long time. Ndomiso, my friend and translator, sat next to me silently and we waited for the other members of the meeting to get comfortable. There was a lot of huffing and puffing and general chitchat in a language I didn't understand as people shifted on the matting, making themselves comfortable.

I had been invited to an elders' meeting in the community of Shewula, situated in north-east Swaziland. It was 2001 and I had been asked to help with the development of much-needed projects in the area. I was relatively new to this and the volunteer company that I was working for at the time was looking for worthwhile projects to support. This took the form of building classrooms, kitchens, community centres, etc.

There I was, sitting on the floor not knowing what to expect. We began the meeting with a prayer (that went well), and then there followed a debate / discussion / joke / catch-up on what they'd all been doing throughout the day. To be honest I had no idea what was going on as it was all in siSwati.

Ndomiso tried to keep pace and summarised each speech for me and gradually the conversation turned to the development of their community. The whole process was drawn-out but I had hoped a decision would be made by the end of the meeting. I was beginning to get the impression that ideas were flowing and the community was happy with our support. We were getting to the fine-tuning of things and by now I was fidgeting – I've never found it comfortable sitting on the floor.

"Food is going to be served," said Ndomiso. I was delighted as I was hungry, although a bit curious as to what was going to be put in front of us. Believe you me, a goat's head was not on my list of what to expect, but there it was, sitting on a platter, looking at me. The goat's head had obviously been boiled, it was sitting skew-whiff on the platter, mouth slightly open, resembling a congealed mess. The elders all looked at me and gesticulated for me to participate in its consumption, I was the guest of honour and they all smiled encouragingly at me. I looked at the goat's head, it looked back at me, tauntingly. There was no way I could get out of this.

I reached toward the platter silently listing the bits of the head that I would rather eat and the bits I would rather not. The tongue came out on top of the list of most edible, so I pried open its jaws and using the knife on the platter cut a slither of its tongue. I popped into my mouth, smiled politely and swallowed quickly. To my surprise, it wasn't too bad at all.

The discussions continued and the platter disappeared into the gloom to my left. I thought I'd seen the last of the goat but a few minutes later it reappeared to my right, this time with a spoon sticking out of the top of its head. My heart sank. It wasn't the fact that I was going to have to eat goat's brains, it was more the fact of how many people had used the spoon previously. When it comes to cooking, I am a pretty hygienic person. I took a spoonful of what could only be described as liquid scrambled egg, smiled sweetly, (although it may have been a grimace), and passed the platter to my left. I wondered how long this purgatory was going to last. Yet again that wretched head appeared. Ndomiso was having an absolute giggle at my expense and in a loud voice reached over me and said, "Here Jenny, try the eyeball, this is a delicacy." Not only was the goat looking at me (from Ndomiso's hand), but all the elders were as well. Luckily, Ndomiso and I went halves on the eyeball so it was small enough for me to swallow whole.

The worst was yet to come. By now the goat's head was pretty mangled and again Ndomiso kindly helped me out. He was really enjoying this.

"This is a tasty morsel for you, Jenny," he said, and proceeded to cut a section of the cheek.

If the goat's head had been roasted or fried it would have been relatively easy to eat. However, as it had been boiled, there were still hairs on the skin. And the hairs were long and tough. As I put it into my mouth I realised that I would not be able to swallow it whole because Ndomiso had obligingly given me a rather large piece. I gagged, recovered my poise, and did my best to chew as quickly as possible. The hairs prickled the inside of my mouth and I gagged again, hoping that no one noticed. I chewed furiously until I swallowed on the third attempt. The goat's head disappeared, thankfully never to be seen again – not by me anyway.

The meeting finished and I was delighted to have several worthwhile projects to work on although, I did wonder whether eating the goat's head was really worth it. As the elders melted into the night, Ndomiso asked me what I thought of the food.

"It was horrible, Ndomiso. I've never had anything so disgusting. Thank you so much for setting me up like that!" Ndomiso fell about laughing and then shouted into the night something I didn't understand in siSwati, but I certainly could make out my name amongst the words.

There was silence and then echoing back came the cackling laughter of some of the elders. "Aaaah, Jeeeny," followed by more laughter and what sounded like thigh-slapping.

A Lunch Too Far

"If I have any more I will vomit," said Zanele. I wholeheartedly agreed; four lunches in three hours was a bit excessive. If I didn't see chicken and rice on my plate for a month I would be delighted.

I was with Charli, Suzy, Alice, and Caislin on a World Vision visit to sponsor the children of St Helen and St Katharine School. Years ago, the school set up a fund to assist four girls through their education from primary school to high school. Every two years the school sends an expedition out to Swaziland and arranges a visit to see the girls.

Early in the morning, we set off to meet Zanele, and our driver, Sipho, who took us on a journey that would stretch from the north-east of Swaziland all the way down to the south, only about 4 hours but that is the full extent of Swaziland. We really were seeing the kingdom in a day.

After a bit of paperwork for security purposes we arrived at the first homestead to visit Nokwazi. She lived in a house that had the most incredible views overlooking rolling mountains and, as Caislin said, "The view could have been painted for a bad movie back drop." She was right, it didn't look real.

Caislin was the representative sponsor for Nokwazi and, along with the food parcels that we had bought for the family, each of the girls had brought a bag with some fun and educational things inside, 'pick up sticks' was a real hit (it's a simple game of picking up a stick without moving any of the others). It was lovely seeing all of the girls engage with Nokwazi and her family. At first everyone was shy but as the day progressed each visit became easier in the sense of talking with the families, playing with the children, learning about the culture, and not feeling so intimidated by entering into people's private homesteads.

Then we thought it was time to go, until we were asked to sit down to eat. Chicken and sweet potatoes emerged and as I was rather hungry I had a second serving as they were so delicious – the best I'd had for a long time. That second potato may have been my downfall. Little did I know what was in store for us all over the next few hours. We all piled back into the vehicle, said our fond farewells, and set off for the next homestead to see Sikhanyiso.

Alice was the person to meet the next sponsored child. Unfortunately, Sikhanyiso was not there, which was a real disappointment. I felt sorry for Alice as she was expecting to see her sponsor child.

However, we met her family as they all benefit from the support. This comprised of her mother, grandmother, and two-month-old baby sister, as well as a guy I think was her grandfather but I was not too sure. Families are very much 'anyone who is remotely related who live in the same place.' Alice immediately had the baby thrust into her arms by Sikhanyiso's mother to say hello. The baby girl looked like a Telly Tubby as she was wrapped up in a light blue onesie with only its dear little face peeking out. No doubt Alice was the first white person she had seen and she took it in her stride. The look on Alice's face was priceless as she was given the baby! I wish I'd captured her astonishment on camera.

We were asked to sit down and then we were presented with another lunch, this time chicken and rice. It is a Swazi tradition to offer guests food, or at least a drink, when entering a homestead. Despite having so little, they give so generously and it was a real honour to sit and eat with the families. You cannot fault the Swazis for their hospitality, this makes the country such a wonderful place to visit.

Then, we went on to a school to pick up Precious, the girl who Suzy was officially visiting. As we arrived, children poured out of the classrooms to meet us and poor Precious was asked to come to the front. Being a shy girl this was obviously embarrassing for her. However, the teacher was having none of that and she was cajoled to come forward and say hello to all of us.

The school that Precious was attending had six classrooms, each classroom with around 20 children, and they all wanted to come out and meet us. I think the donation from the girls not only goes to the families of each sponsored child but also to community projects as well, so all these children were benefiting from the money that was being sent over each year. Everyone wanted to have their picture taken!

The head teacher gave Precious permission to leave early, and she clambered into the vehicle with us. Precious was nine years old, but small for her age and extremely reserved, I think she was simply overwhelmed by being in a vehicle full of white people. She was certainly more comfortable when we got to her home.

At Precious's house we were greeted by more plates of chicken and rice. *When will it ever end?* I silently asked myself. I knew it was rude not to eat any of it and I did my best to plough through the mountain of rice in front of me. It was obviously a big occasion for them to have visitors as the neighbours had been invited to join in the dining. More people kept turning up, and they greeted us as we struggled to eat everything. The free-range chicken was tasty, albeit a bit tough. It had probably been running around the yard that morning.

Suzy had brought a frisbee and this was a real hit. I don't think Precious knew what a frisbee was. Why should she? It isn't a common item in Swaziland. So, Suzy and Caislin demonstrated how to throw a frisbee, albeit not well to begin with which provided a huge amount of entertainment for the rest of us as well as all the family. Eventually the girls managed to throw it properly and Precious was integrated into the activity.

Suzy had also bought some lovely gifts for Precious, one of which was nail varnish. This was an absolute hit. What a brilliant idea, and Precious's face simply lit up like a beacon when Suzy put some on her fingernails.

Finally, we jumped into the car for our visit to Nomile. We had heard that her homestead had caught fire, and later found out that a candle had been knocked over and burnt Nomile's bed, blankets, most of her clothes, and destroyed some of the family's essential possessions. Luckily, we had found this out before we set out and had brought some blankets to replace the ones that she had lost. We gave gifts of food, and toys for the children, met the family, and learnt a small part about their lives. Charli had brought an excellent pop-up book that caught everyone's imagination, more so the adults than the children!

I think we were all secretly glad there was no sign of any food. Until, from nowhere, and I mean nowhere, there appeared... you guessed it... a plate of chicken and rice for each of us. It was rather embarrassing trying to eat my fourth plate of food in the hope that I didn't overdo it, but not leave too much in case we caused offence.

On the way back to the main road, after travelling for hours on dirt tracks, we managed to track down Sikhanyiso, who we later discovered was staying with her grandmother. Finding her grandmother's house proved to be a tricky challenge, but after asking at several houses we eventually found her. Alice was delighted to be able to meet Sikhanyiso, as was I. To begin with Sikhanyiso was shy; she was only five years old, and having someone translating for her didn't really work. She was so overawed by the experience she was monosyllabic. Alice had the brilliantly imaginative idea to converse with Sikhanyiso through pictures drawn in the dust, and they spent forty-five minutes hunkered in the dirt drawing pictures of cats, stars, and other objects that I couldn't fathom.

That day was a special one; we were so warmly welcomed into each homestead that it felt as if we were part of each family too. It was a day away from tourism and a chance to experience something that not that many people have the incredible opportunity to do.

Now, where are my indigestion tablets?

The Honey Badger and my Steak

When in Africa, you must participate in a braai, even if you just do the eating. The word braai means to grill or roast meat over open coals and is the shortened word of *braavleis*, which means *cookery* in Afrikaans.

The Africans, especially Zimbabweans and South Africans, have got the creation of a barbecue down to a tee, and they are also good at telling you that this is the case. Unfortunately, I have to admit that they are right. We British cannot create a decent barbeque for toffee. We struggle to set the barbeque alight in the first place and end up dousing the whole thing and ourselves in so much lighter fluid that I am surprised we do not poison or burn ourselves more often than we already do. We don't leave the coals alight for long enough, we put too much or too little fuel on the fire, we put the food on too early while it is still a flaming inferno, (which results in a burnt crisp outer shell and raw meat in the middle), and then we leave those wonderful coals burning at their prime, whilst we sit around saying how delicious our food is. We stick religiously to sausages, beef burgers, and chicken legs, and then put them in nasty white rolls adorned with limp lettuce. And, of course, it will probably rain. There is so much more to a braai, it is a religion in southern Africa.

I have learnt the hard way. Large South Africans have taken cooking implements away from me with a look of disgust as I did everything wrong, and I mean everything. I even stood wrong.

The variety of food that can go on a braai is endless; T-bone steaks, boervros (sausages), impala steak, butternut filled with feta cheese and wrapped in foil, normal sausages, chops, spatchcock chicken, fillet of something else, prawns, mushrooms, ribs, all with great marinades. But I think the most important thing for your braai is the location – everything tastes better under a starlit sky and with the sounds of African wildlife making music for your ears.

The best steak I have had was in Etosha National Park in Namibia. I love Etosha – the shimmering mirages over the salt pans, springbok daintily walking through the grass, herds of wildebeest on an endless horizon, and an air of expectancy – you never know what you're going to see or experience.

I remember the first time I went to Etosha, which

was over two decades ago, and I was blown away by the scenery. It was in January and I'd managed to escape the winter blues of the UK to the very, *very* sunny climate of Namibia. I was in my element.

I had a few days off, which I decided to spend in Etosha. I packed my car with my camping gear and headed north. Back in those days the camps in Etosha were a little shabby and DIY camping was often considered a better option. I bought some firewood and the necessities for a braai – tinfoil, potatoes, garlic, onion, courgettes, and a juicy steak.

I was really excited about spending some time in Etosha and I had been advised to stay at Halali, a camp in the middle of Etosha, as it would be quieter and the waterhole would have more wildlife. I bought a map of the reserve and meticulously marked a route to get there by sunset.

I had a wonderful game drive that day and saw: a lion drinking from a waterhole; a pair of cheetahs; a host of elephants; and what seemed like thousands of springbok glimmering in the distance.

When I arrived at Halali I was delighted to find hardly anyone there, as I was looking forward to a peaceful night's sleep. When I drove into the campsite I discovered that I was the only person camping – the other few residents were staying in the camp huts. At that time, the site in Halali was a large expanse of dry, baked earth, with a few trees to provide shade and a couple of ablution blocks. There was nobody around at all.

I was pretty content with this and got the braai lit and left it to create coals as I set up my tent and organised myself. Once this was done I sat next to the fire, sipping my beer, waiting for the embers to be just right for my juicy T-bone steak. My mouth was watering already in anticipation. Soon enough, it was time to cook.

It was at this point that I realised I wasn't the only living thing in the camp, and my companion was also interested in my steak. I had been discovered by the resident honey badger, who had appeared to check me out.

Honey badgers are not that large, but they are renowned for being ferocious and fearless, which are not characteristics that I possess. This tough little creature has a stocky, flattened body with short, strong legs, along with long claws on the front feet for digging and defence. The honey badger's hair is thick and coarse, mostly black, with a wide, grey-white stripe that stretches across its back from the top of its head to the tip of its tail.

The honey badger also has a gland at the base of its tail that stores a stinky liquid just as powerful as that of its look-alike, the skunk. The smelly stuff is used to mark territory, but if the honey badger is frightened or threatened, it drops a stink bomb (rather than spraying like a skunk). The honey badger's odour doesn't last long, but it still gets its message across: "Leave me alone. Don't mess with me!"

After stealing a dinner from bees or taking a sting from one of the world's deadliest snakes, the puff adder, the average honey badger briefly sleeps it off. The venom from a puff adder is powerful enough to melt human skin. Just another reason why the honey badger gets his tough-guy reputation, and why I was a bit concerned about my welfare, my steak, and whether I was going to smell a stink bomb that evening.

He snaked his way over to me and had a good look at my tent. There was nothing of interest there. Then he had a look in the nearby bin and was temporarily distracted by the ends of courgettes and a bit of onion. But not for long, the sizzling steak seemed to be of interest, or maybe it was me standing next to the steak?

I stepped gingerly away from the steak (at this point I was more concerned about the welfare of my steak than the presence of the beast), although I still had a healthy wariness for this creature. My car was parked nearby and I used this as a shield, keeping the car between me and the badger.

He approached. He poked his head around the side of the car and looked at me, I kept moving around the car, and he kept following me. I was acutely aware that my steak was on the braai and made sure that I could see both my steak and the honey badger.

There then ensued a comedy moment. We circled warily, keeping each other in our sights whilst circumnavigating the car three times. Each time I passed the braai I checked my steak was okay before moving on. In hindsight this was utterly ridiculous – who runs around the car with a honey badger chasing them? I could have got into the car, the animal could have crawled under the car, or it could have taken my steak if it had really wanted to. Luckily, there is no CCTV in Halali campsite!

The honey badger did eventually depart, (he'd probably got bored with going round and round in circles), and I was left with a perfect evening under a starlit sky, a story to recount, and an excellent steak to devour.

Biltong is like Marmite

Biltong – *you either love it or hate it*. And I love it. But then I am a bit of a carnivore and I will devour cured meats of any kind.

Folklore has it that migrating tribesmen, herding their stock, would place strips of venison under the saddles on their horses so the chaffing would tenderise the meat and the sweat of the animals would spice it. I'm not too sure whether this is true or not but it doesn't sound appetising.

The word *biltong* is from the Dutch *bil* (rump) and *tong* (strip, or tongue). It is dried meat that originated from the pioneering Voortrekkers in South Africa and has a much more credible European history than that of African tribesmen. As these explorers migrated by wagon from the Cape Colony to the north-east of South Africa (and away from the British), they needed stocks of durable food for their journey. Biltong was created out of necessity for these travellers as they moved across the continent.

The meat was preserved using a blend of vinegar, salt, sugar, coriander, and other spices, and hung out to dry in the sun. These preservatives were in abundance in the Cape Colony, as French Hugenots produced wine and vinegar from their grape crops and the colony was the half-way stop for seafarers plying the eastern spice routes. Once dry, the biltong was packed into cloth bags and stacked into their wagons. It was an easy and effective way to store meat for prolonged periods of time, prevented flies laying their eggs on fresh meat, and stopped the meat from rotting in the intense heat.

Nowadays, many different types of meat are used to produce biltong ranging from beef and game animals to fillets of ostrich. It is typically made from raw strips of meat that are dipped in vinegar and then rubbed with salt and a variety of dried herbs and spices. Coriander seeds are a common spice used. The strips of meat are then hung and left to dry for about four days, or until ready to eat.

The first time I ate biltong was on a journey through Zimbabwe and we had bought some 'wet' biltong. *Wet* biltong means that the meat has not been dried all the way through and is still soft in the middle, whereas normal run-of-the-mill biltong is completely dry and can be brittle and tough to chew. Dry biltong is even used as a teething aid for babies, although I wouldn't recommend it.

I immediately loved the taste and texture of wet biltong, but a limit was imposed on me as to how much I could eat. This was not because I was going to demolish the whole lot, although that was a definite possibility, but simply because there is a lot of chewing involved. Eating too much biltong, if you are not used to it, can result in serious jaw ache! I did moan about this, eat too much, and promptly got jaw ache, but it was worth every minute of the ensuing agony.

Biltong can be bought in most southern African

supermarkets and it is often sold at the tobacco kiosk at the entrance to supermarkets. This is because it is a popular snack and you can purchase your biltong without having to go into the shop and battle through the aisles of rice, mealie meal, and powdered soups. However, I think the best biltong can be bought from stalls near a butcher's, or game farms. As you are driving through southern Africa you often find meat stalls by the side of the road outside game and cattle farms. Each one will have its only family secret recipe and rivalry is often evident between different farms.

The one place where I don't seem to be able to find decent biltong is in Swaziland; instead I resort to dry wors – dried sausage, cured in the same fashion as biltong but less chewy and easier on the jaw, so I can eat as much as I like in one sitting.

I remember the first time I made biltong. I was given an impala carcass from a cull. It had been dumped on my doorstep and, as I hadn't got enough room in the freezer, I decided to make biltong. Admittedly, I did have some advice and help on how to make it, and it wasn't something I embarked upon lightly. I knew I had to skin the impala, cut the meat into strips of the correct thickness, put the right combination of vinegar and spices onto the meat, and then hang them up to dry away from flies and opportunistic scavengers such as jackals and rats. And it had to be done the same day.

Luckily, I had been advised to skin and gut the impala outside in my garden, which resembled the bush, otherwise the kitchen would have got messy and might even have attracted unwanted visitors inside. To begin with I strung the impala up from a tree, which required a lot of effort, so that it would be easier to skin. I meticulously removed the skin without puncturing the stomach cavity. If I had cut into any of the digestive tract the contents of the intestines could taint a considerable amount of the meat rendering it disgusting. As this was only my second attempt at skinning an impala, and this time I was by myself, I made sure I was careful with my blade.

I eventually removed the skin, although this took longer than I had anticipated, and I stood back to admire my handiwork. I think any butcher would have been horrified by the result. It looked as if a werewolf had attacked the antelope leaving a mauled carcass, flayed skin, and stomach contents strewed all over the ground. It was not a pretty sight, and neither was I with smears of blood across my shorts and over my brow. I looked as if I had walked out of one of the Texas Chainsaw Massacre films.

I carved off sections of meat, took them into the kitchen and cut them into various-sized strips. The strips were certainly not uniform in size but I had been assured that this meant the biltong would dry at different rates giving me a mixture of wet and dry biltong. This part of the process was easy although time-consuming. I dipped each strip of meat in vinegar and then into my spices. I chose coriander and black pepper, partly because I thought it would be tasty with this combination and partly because they were the only ones that I possessed at the time.

I hung the meat using clothes pegs, (which I

didn't use again for the purpose for which they were designed), on a makeshift washing line that criss-crossed my veranda. My veranda surrounded the outside of my house and was enclosed by mosquito netting and was therefore an excellent place for my biltong to dry. I saw the reason for the vinegar – it kept some fat, blue flies, (with bulbous red eyes), off my tasty snacks.

Each morning I would get up to check the firmness of my biltong and see how the curing was progressing. It was only three days later that some were ready to eat and I can proudly say the end result was delicious. This time there was no one there to stop me from getting jaw ache –consequently I had an aching jaw for two months, continuously! They kept me going on my long days out in the bush.

I would advise everyone to try biltong, (unless you're vegetarian), as it is part of the culture. If you want to 'taste' Africa, then biltong is the way to go.

Maputo Fish Market

Entering Maputo Fish Market in Mozambique, I was overcome by the intensity of the fish sellers, the glorious quantity and variety of fish and shellfish on sale, and the fact that my world had immediately reduced to the fish stalls. No longer was I aware of the busy and hectic lifestyle of the 1.4 million people outside in the city, nor was I conscious of vehicles hooting and tooting maniacally at each other. My focus was on large bowls of fresh cockles occasionally with water squirting over the side from siphons.

I have been to many fish markets but Maputo's stands out in my mind. I'm always impressed by the way the fish and shellfish are laid out to entice prospective buyers: prawns lined up and facing the same way in military style; squid with their tentacles all pointing to one corner; cockles glistening in ceramic bowls; and large fish nestling in ice, looking as if they are holding their breath they look so fresh. You can guarantee that the fish have been pulled from the sea within the last twenty-four hours, even more recently than that.

At the fish market, you are spoilt for choice. The catch of the day on offer might include; various varieties of fish, mussels, lobster, crabs, langoustines, or prawns. There are also traders selling cashew nuts and various arts and crafts aimed at the tourists. It is a delight to behold.

I once made a trip to Maputo Fish Market before flying back home. My flight was a few hours away and, being a Sunday, most restaurants seemed to be closed, but luckily the fish market never sleeps.

The entrance into Maputo Fish Market does not do it justice. It's a rusty, corrugated archway surrounded by dilapidated buildings in a run-down side street leading away from the ocean front. Before even entering the market you are pounced upon by street vendors and hawkers trying to sell you cashews, batteries, and car-watching services; there was even someone trying to sell me a shovel. I didn't want to put that in my hand luggage! Once I'd managed to navigate through this wave of entrepreneurs, I entered the gloom of the market.

The large area selling fish is covered, I presume to prevent the produce from drying out and losing its appeal. The area was much cooler than outside, due to all the ice being used to keep the food fresh, and the floor was awash with melted water mingled with raw fish. I made sure I walked around the whole market, which took some time, before making a decision on what I was going to buy. I was beginning to salivate already at the prospect of dining on the food extravaganza in front of my eyes.

The starter was a no-brainer; I always have cockles, a mixture of the larger, meatier ones and the smaller, more delicate ones. I bought the equivalent of one can of cockles, which was thrown into a plastic bag and handed over the counter to me. However, there was too much choice for my main course. After a lot of deliberation I went for squid, which was rather surprising as I normally choose prawns. Six small squid were selected and again they were thrown into a plastic bag after being weighed. I did check that ice had not been surreptitiously added to increase the weight – a sneaky little trick that some of the sellers try to increase the weight of a purchase. It has happened to me before.

In the old days there was an independent weigher who would weigh your bag for 10 meticals, (about 0.001p, but that currency is no longer in use). You could check it with the stall owner to see if you had been fleeced. Once, when I was walking over to the official weigher, I realised that there was an awful lot of water in the bag, so I punched some holes in the bottom and let the water trickle out as I walked, slowly, for my prawns to be re-weighed. Of course it was now lighter than the seller had stated, so there was a lot of shouting and gesticulating until a fair price was agreed upon.

Once I'd purchased my cockles and squid I proudly walked around the back of the fish market into the leisurely sea of people eating their Sunday lunch. There was a plethora of different colours of tables and chairs with eager waiters around them. I chose a red table and chairs under an umbrella and was approached by the owner. The great thing about Maputo Fish Market is that you can have your purchase cooked on site with a rustic restaurant feel to it.

I handed over my plastic bag of cockles and squid and asked for chips with them, no salad, and a 2M beer (pronounced 'dosh-em') which is the local brew, and tasty it is too. Don't go for the salad as it is often washed in the local water and Maputo's water and sewage system can be a rather hit and miss affair. There is something surreal about sitting at a picnic table, surrounded by fish sellers, having passed over a dubious plastic bag full of fish and waiting for the food to be returned in spectacularly edible form.

Whatever you do, don't even think of going into the kitchen to check on the progress of your food or to keep an eye on the quantity being cooked. The kitchens are so basic you will probably wonder how any food can be produced hygienically at all. The preparation is simple with everything grilled over charcoal or fried. You can't hurry perfection. Don't go if you're in a hurry, time slows down to the pace of a cockle race. It is worth waiting for.

The cockles came cooked in a broth of celery, parsley, and garlic, and they were garnished with lemon wedges – absolutely divine. Eating with your fingers makes the whole experience even more enjoyable. I leisurely picked every single cockle out and slurped up most of the juice. I did suspect that more salt had been added than was needed to the broth to try and make me order more drinks. However, I had my own trusty water bottle to save the day.

The main course of squid came on a platter with garlic and chilli, and each squid had been scored meticulously to ensure the flavour ran through the whole dish. Calamari at their greatest. The chips were obviously homemade and had a rustic texture – the perfect accompaniment to my lunch.

I had taken so much time in eating my cockles and squid and become so immersed with the way of life in the fish market that I only just made it to the airport on time. Naturally, I slept well on the flight home.

A visit to Maputo Fish Market is a truly memorable experience: the food is out of this world and the ambience is extraordinary – but do keep one eye on the clock!

TOUCH

There are a number of experiences that I have had which highlight different 'touches' whilst I've been in Africa. Although you'll doubtless have an incredible desire to touching the animals you see, I do not encourage people to do so. The reason for this is that allowing wild animals to get accustomed and habituated to humans is not healthy, can cause conflict or the transfer of disease, and in serious cases nasty injuries or fatalities. The best thing is simply to watch these animals go about their business in a natural environment.

However, like anyone, I have leapt at the opportunity to have contact with wild animals, under the right, or lucky, circumstances.

Unexpected Guests

Dave, Lori, and I were sitting around the fire in Mlilwane, Swaziland, enjoying our after-meal drinks and doing a spot of star gazing. Lori was not too keen on the creepy crawlies, so I had planned the trip to be in Swaziland's winter, when no self-respecting bug would be seen out in the cold. It can also be a quiet time in Swaziland so we practically had the camp to ourselves. Dave, Lori, and I, were the only people sitting out that night. It was wonderfully quiet.

Out of the corner of my eye I caught some movement, there was something out there in the black night. In Mlilwane camp wildlife roams free and often there are night-time visitors including nyala, impalas, zebras, and hippos. We waited, holding our breath. Then three warthogs appeared from the inky blackness, a large mother with her two only-slightly-smaller offspring approaching us without a care in the world. The tusks on the mother were enormous and I curled my legs under myself, as it felt safer!

"Don't move," I said. "They are coming into our space not the other way round, so make no sudden movements."

We watched with anticipation. What happened next took me completely by surprise, as it did Dave, who has travelled nearly as extensively as I have in Africa.

One of the younger warthogs, which was still the size of a large labrador and sporting impressive tusks, pushed Dave's feet out of the way with its snout, dug a small hollow in the ground and promptly lay down next to the fire to keep warm. This was obviously their bedroom for the night and we were in it. The second warthog snuggled itself next to its brother and lay his head gently on Lori's foot. The mother took stock of the situation, eyed me up and down, and then went to bed on the other side of the fire, keeping a close watch. I don't think any of us breathed for a minute.

We sat there for a while with our mouths wide open, revelling in this exceptionally close contact with wildlife s, in Lori's case actual contact, before finishing our drinks and quietly creeping off leaving our hogs snoozing by the fire.

It Does Get Cold in Africa

I am often surprised to hear that people think it is always hot in Africa, this is far from the truth. It can get exceptionally cold at night, especially in southern Africa, and it snows in Africa too. Both northern and southern Africa experience cold winters with frequent frosts, as well as the more predicable hot summers.

In the UK, we frequently talk about the weather; in fact we are obsessed by the subject, and we will discuss all aspects of our climate. In Africa, people are more focused on whether it is dry or wet, rather than how hot it is. Rain is a crucial part of the way of life and critical to many people's livelihood.

During one African winter I was pleasantly surprised to discover a hot water bottle in my bed while staying at one of the lodges in Swaziland. I'll admit I was not expecting that, so it was rather a shock when I got into bed. At first I thought it was a dangerous furry animal residing in there, unnaturally over-heating to a deathly temperature and also inanimate.

There have been many stories of lodge guests stabbing hot water bottles in fear of retaliation, the result being a wet bed, an embarrassed guest, and a terminally-ill hot water bottle.

Africa has a winter, although maybe not to the degree of low temperatures that we experience in the UK. You do have to be smart when packing for a safari, especially when it's during their winter months, as it can be chilly at night and early in the morning on game drives.

I particularly remember a morning game drive in

Botswana during April. We were advised to dress warmly. We were camping in Moremi Game Reserve, which borders the Okavango Delta, and the temperature that night had been particularly cold. I'd even worn my woolly hat in bed. When I pitched up for the safari with woolly hat, fleeces, and my sleeping bag, I got strange looks and a few sniggers from my fellow travellers. However, shortly after we set off, I was the one laughing (not too loudly), as I sat snug as a bug in my sleeping bag, nice and toasty warm, while the others braved the inclement temperature. Halfway through the drive I emerged from my cocoon, just as everyone else was defrosting.

I enjoy winter in Africa because it means cold nights, which makes sleeping easy. It also means cooler, crisper days, and bright, blue skies – excellent for photography. It's often shorts and T-shirt weather during the day, but of course the days are shortened.

The colder weather also keeps the crawling bugs and flying insects, such as mosquitoes, at bay and no self-respecting snake will come out in the cold. If you are concerned about bugs, creepy crawlies, snakes, and malaria, then it is advisable to travel during Africa's winter months.

Make sure you are aware of the likely temperatures during your stay. A woolly hat is advisable, along with a warm fleece for the evenings, and some warm trousers just in case there is a cold snap and you are caught unawares. There's nothing like sitting round an open fire under the African stars, toasting your feet, and listening to the noises of the bush.

Life on Game Capture

I spent a happy month working with a game capture unit. I was living in the bush, manhandling animals of all shapes and sizes, loading them in and out of crates, and driving them across the wilderness.

I was certainly thrown in at the deep end, finding myself feeding captured rhinos while they were in their crates; walking in a line through the bush trying not to step on any unsuspecting snakes; picking ticks off my overalls by the dozen; and rugby-tackling antelope before injecting them with a sedative. It was the stuff that dreams are made of.

It was also incredibly hard work. We were getting up before the sun rose and, after a quick breakfast, we were on the move through the bush for the whole day. There was no time for those who could not keep up and if you made a mistake you certainly knew about it. Take any one of our tasks and there was scope for serious injury or mishap.

The most enjoyable time I had was capturing nyala. While this lacked the adventure of using a helicopter, chasing semi-sedated giraffe in vehicles across bumpy terrain, or watching rhinos being manoeuvred from one crate to another, nyala capture held plenty of excitement as it is all done by hand. Nyala are dense-bush-dwelling antelope and as a result cannot be rounded up by vehicle or helicopter. Instead a large net about 3m high and 30m long is set up in the bush, in an area where nyala are known to frequent. Then, a handful of people called spotters, which often included myself, hide in the bush in front of the net, and wait. You must be incredibly patient to do this as you can be waiting for hours before the action starts. And any movement can alert nearby game.

Meanwhile, a few kilometres away, the rest of the team form a long line and start beating the bush to flush out the antelope and push them towards the trap. At this point my adrenalin levels were normally overloaded as I could hear the game moving nearer to our hiding spot. As the animals get closer the tendency to hold your breath gets greater and I found that my senses, especially my hearing and sight, were heightened. Then, a dozen or so nyala would run past me, so close that I could touch them, and fall into the netting. Then the action began for us spotters.

Immediately, we would be upon the animals bringing them physically to the ground, lying across them and blindfolding them. If a nyala didn't hit the netting it was a bit of a free for all. They would be rugby-tackled to the ground. Lying on the animals and blindfolding them would calm them down (although it might not sound that way), and would prevent them from hurting themselves. At this point a vet would sedate them to prevent further stress. Once sedated, you could walk the nyala as if you are pushing a bicycle, one hand on an ear and the other hand grabbing the hair on its shoulder, and you could steer it towards the truck or container. A very odd experience all round!

I had a wonderful time working alongside a game capture team. You never knew what type of game might hit the net. Generally, it was nyala, but we did once have a rather unhappy leopard. We decided to leave her to untangle herself!

That night we were based at a farmstead. The owners obviously cared passionately about animals because there were rescue animals of all shapes and sizes living in the house, ranging from wild cats to meerkats – all things fluffy and cuddly, and I fell in love with the place.

It may not seem much, but I was asked to look after the new addition, a meerkat, a small bundle of fluff that needed constant supervision and to be kept warm. I was offered this important role and the tiny male pup instantly became attached to me, and me to it. Meerkats go round in groups called a mob, gang, or clan, and I like to think I became part of his gang, with him tucked into my fleece to keep off the chill of the cold mornings.

Meerkats are intriguing animals, they can dig their own body weight of dirt in a couple of seconds, they are immune to the poison of snakes and scorpions, and they are such good hunters that some have been tamed to become rodent catchers. However, they are the favourite food of eagles and hawks and with a sharp shrill from one of the meerkat sentries the whole clan will disappear into their burrow network. Young meerkats are so afraid of predatory birds that even airplanes will send them diving for cover.

That was where I came in. I protected this bundle of joy from airborne threats, kept him warm from the harsh weather, and spoke to him as a team member. It was a joy that only lasted for two days but provided memories for a lifetime.

You never forget when a wild animal accepts you into its pack, whatever its size.

Handling Poo – The Art of Tracking

I always find it amusing when I'm with a new group who watch me for the first time as I bend down and pick up some animal poo. The reactions are mixed.

There are those who look in utter amazement and then crowd forward to see what I'm holding in my hands. There are those who turn their nose up at the thought of handling faeces, but still have that inkling of curiosity to see why I am doing it. And there are those who recoil in horror, take a few backward steps and tell me how disgusting I am. Whichever group you are in, I can guarantee that by the end of your trip to Africa you will have held, in your unprotected hands, some animal poo.

It's not that I do this for the shock value, (although my inner self is having a bit of a giggle), but it is part of the all-encompassing educational nature of being in Africa – the art of tracking wildlife in the bush. You can learn a lot by picking up animal faeces and examining it.

I would say, however, that picking up dry faeces is much more agreeable than the wet kind. The wetter the faeces the nearer you are to the animal. You can tell from the shape of the faeces which animal it belongs to, or at least which group of animals. Large, melon-sized balls are probably from a rhino, elephant, or maybe hippo. Raisin-sized droppings (often found in a pile), are likely to be from social antelopes. Elongated, twisted faeces about the size of your thumb, are more likely to be from carnivores, and large, kidney-bean shapes are probably zebras. Just having a rudimentary idea of these shapes can help you out.

Look at the scattering of the poo. Giraffe droppings have a long way to drop, and they often bounce all over the place, whereas eland poo has less distance to fall and is therefore more likely to be found in a neat pile. So, the distribution can help determine the animal as well.

Also, look at the environment that you are in. For instance, if you're on a wide-open plain and you're looking at a melon-sized ball of poo, it is unlikely to be that of a black rhino. Black rhino prefer dense vegetation to open bushveld. Alternatively, if you find smaller, raisin-sized droppings, which are probably from an antelope, you could assume that they would be unlikely to belong to a springbok or impala as they prefer open spaces, and more likely be from either a nyala or bushbuck.

Having further knowledge of the distribution of specific animals makes life easier as well. For example, puku and red lechwe are antelope that are only found in the north of Botswana, black rhino have a specific distribution, and you are more likely to come across cheetah in Namibia than anywhere else in Africa.

There is so much you can learn from looking at faeces – you just need to know what you are looking for. To get the real nitty-gritty you will have to pick up the faeces, look at it closely, carefully tear it apart and look at what is inside.

The classic example is recognising the difference between an elephant, a white rhino, a black rhino, and a hippo. Hippo are pretty easy because, although they eat grass, (as do white rhino), they often use their tail to spread their dung around so most of it is suspended in bushes and trees. Hippo faeces will also be found near water sources, whereas white rhino will be out in the open bush. It will also comprise dried grass.

The real test comes between black rhino and elephants. They feed on similar vegetation, they are both browsers (they eat leaves and twigs), although at times elephants will also consume grass. Elephants are prone to stripping bark so you may see long strands of undigested bark in their faeces if you look carefully. The main thing to look out for is the way in which the twigs are cut in the faeces. Elephants will rip and tear at twigs and small branches, leaving a rough, jagged end to the twigs. Whereas black rhino will cut the twigs at a 45° angle with their back teeth. When you are teasing apart the faeces, keep an eye out for cleanly cut small twigs, with a neat, angled cut, as this will help you identify between a black rhino and an elephant. If that is the case, keep an eye out for a suitable tree to climb. Black rhinos are renowned for being rather feisty.

Where to put all this knowledge to proper and effective use? Being an ecologist by profession, I always like to put my knowledge into practice and help with conservation projects.

I set up a particularly interesting project in Mbuluzi Game Reserve in Swaziland for a group of students. Our project was to collect giraffe dung, and then send it to the USA. Posting poo was a first for me! There was a reason for this – we were helping to determine the genetic makeup of each giraffe on the reserve to help the manager, Tal, to decide which giraffe to keep and which to transfer to a different area, or even move out completely. It would help to prevent inbreeding and would increase the genetic viability of the current population.

Off we went to find the giraffe. You would have thought that finding giraffe would be relatively easy, given their size, but not so. These tall animals blend into the bush with ease. Many times, we drove around the reserve for hours not seeing a single giraffe, and I knew there were over twenty of them in the one small section we were surveying. We were on a tight schedule and only had four days to collect droppings from as many giraffes as possible.

On finding a group of giraffes, (known as a 'tower' if they are stationary and a 'journey' if they are moving), there was a mass of activity. Someone identified each one by its unique features such as skin patterns, or injury (to check that we had not surveyed it already), another took detailed notes if it was a new giraffe, someone else took photos to relate to the notes, and someone else was on poo-watch. We had to be 100% certain that we collected dung from a correctly identified giraffe; anything other than absolute certainty was not acceptable.

We waited for our subject to drop their brown gold, but you can't get a giraffe to poo on demand, so it was often a long while for the next one to come along. Therefore, we had to follow the journey of giraffes into the bush until the one we wanted did its business. Many times we waited expectantly, clutching a brown envelope and a pair of surgical gloves, only to come away with nothing. Sometimes we followed giraffe for an hour through dense bush and only had scratches and torn clothes as evidence of our hard work.

Oh, the joy we experienced when our target giraffe pooed! Our plop-spotter kept the drop zone in sight and directed the collector to the correct location. Finding the faeces was also a challenge, as the pellets often fell into dense grass that reached waist-high. It was particularly difficult rummaging through the undergrowth trying to find it. On finding the pellets the collector confirmed that it was the right sample from the target giraffe, by its freshness and warmth. Picking up poo has its moments!

I must say that there was something incredibly rewarding about having several envelopes stuffed with muck at the end of a working day. Over the four days we managed to identify twenty-one giraffes and collected from eleven of them. Not a mean feat, considering that the Florida students who were analysing the results only managed to see ten giraffes in two weeks.

On the last day, we also managed to get poo from 'Taylor Swift', (she was recorded as giraffe #1, who we saw regularly but had proved to be a bit elusive with her bowel movements).

Job done!

Now, I'd better wash my hands...

Camera! Action! Oops!

Mlilwane Wildlife Sanctuary in Swaziland; Terry, Vicky, and I were enjoying the peace and tranquillity of the reserve. There is something about Mlilwane that makes me feel as if I have come home, it is a wonderful place where you can get away from everybody and take time out for yourself.

We were driving around the park, looking at the animals that were housed in the endangered species breeding area. Ted Reilly, who set up Mlilwane after recognising the demise of Swaziland's wildlife, is re-introducing species that were once roaming wild in the kingdom. We had already seen red duiker, (a small antelope that looks more like a bunny hopping amongst the undergrowth), we'd watched sedentary eland, and heard the booming calls of the blue crane. My best-remembered sighting was that of a roan antelope.

"Stop! Stop! I'd like to take a photo," said Terry, and I pulled the car over to watch the approaching roan.

Terry had his camera on full zoom trying to focus on the animal, and it obliged by walking closer to us.

And closer.

And closer.

Until the roan filled his viewfinder. Terry took his camera away from his face only to realise that the roan was eyeballing him, only 1m away! This did not stop the brazen animal, it leaned towards the open window and stuck its head right into the car and began to nibble on the wing mirror adjuster knob. I was speechless, until I realised that its horns could get caught inside the car. This could not only get messy but the rental company would not be happy.

With some gentle verbal persuasion, the antelope removed its head from our vehicle, licked the wing mirror as a passing shot, and nonchalantly walked off to graze on something more wholesome, like grass. Terry never got his award-winning picture, the roan was far too close and had steamed up his lens. He was too busy laughing to concentrate on taking a photo anyway.

I'm Not a 'Cat Person', but I'll make an Exception Now and Then

Sometimes the opportunity to touch an animal arises in a controlled environment, and if this is the case, then it will probably touch your heart. I've been exceptionally lucky to have some extraordinary experiences with wildlife through my work as an ecologist, as an expedition leader, and whilst working for a game capture unit.

During my time in Africa I have had an elephant snuffle my ear, an ostrich peck my hand, I have manhandled nyala, rubbed down a hippo, had spiders run over my knees, and had a monkey hold my finger, each one a memorable experience. However, what follows is a remarkable event that I treasure most highly.

My first tactile wild cat experience was having a fully grown male caracal curl up and fall asleep in my lap. Caracals are the cats with pointy ears with black tufts, resembling a lynx. Why was this rare cat snuggling on my lap without a care in the world?

While I was working with a game capture unit in South Africa, I stayed in a beautiful lodge where the owners had an incredible affinity with wildlife. This particular caracal had been brought in to be cared for due to an injury it had sustained on the reserve. It was going to be released back into the wild when fully healed. I was truly enjoying the novelty factor of dozing with a caracal. They are commonly known as the Persian lynx or African lynx, despite the fact that they are not lynx at all, and evolved two million years before the lynx.

A caracal is a large cat to have sitting on your lap, and I quickly came to appreciate the size of it the longer it remained. I was beginning to get pins and needles. These cats are tenacious hunters and they have been known to bring down an ostrich, the fact that they can keep up with one is surprising in itself. However, caracal mainly hunt rodents, birds (which it can catch in flight by leaping into the air), antelopes, gazelles, and rabbits. They possess twenty muscles in their ears allowing them to detect prey from all around and that allows them to become extremely effective hunters. But this one was living the life of Riley, being hand-fed cubes of impala.

I spent two days with this beautiful animal, feeding it, allowing it to sit on my lap, and letting it curl around my legs. However, all good things come to an end and my new furry friend was soon put into a large holding cage to allow him to get used to his natural surroundings – as opposed to a sofa, blanket, and prepared steak.

Incredibly, after two weeks, he apparently had no

memory of his past luxurious life and his friend – he hissed threateningly at me from the back of the cage, ears back, tail up, and teeth bared. This behaviour is specific to caracal. They are adaptable creatures and inherently wild by nature. A week later, he was released back into the wild fully recovered, having completely forgotten about impala steaks, a secure bed, a comfy lap, and little ol' me. He might have forgotten me but I certainly won't forget him.

I really am not a cat person but they do seem to like me. Normal moggies seem to find my lap attractive, as do the not-so-normal ones, like when I woke up to find a cheetah lying across my feet.

It was 6am and I was woken by the maid calling my name as she brought tea into my room. I'd had a rather uncomfortable night and ascertained the reason once I saw the cheetah lying across my feet rendering my legs numb. The maid seemed unbothered by the whole thing, she smiled at me and said good morning and left me to fend for myself. I peered over the sheets, holding my bedding in a white-knuckle death grip and looked at my bedfellow. Obviously this was normal behaviour, the maid had not batted an eyelid, but what was I supposed to do? The cheetah made my decision for me (thankfully, as I was at a loss). He looked at me, yawned, stretched, flexed his claws and leisurely hauled himself off my feet and nonchalantly walked out of the room without a care in the world.

A cup of sweet tea was in order while the feeling returned to my legs and I regained composure.

Even more thrilling was another experience with

the same cheetah. I was conducting some research into cheetah projects in Namibia and found myself visiting a farm that took in problem cheetahs. These cheetahs had, more often than not, killed cattle and were therefore considered pests. The cheetahs were captured and relocated to a farm in the north of Namibia where they were fed and looked after and, if possible, new homes were found for them.

I arrived by car and got out to open the gates. There was a fenced area, as with all homesteads, where the land around the house is protected from wild animals getting too near to the home. Just as I was opening the gates I noticed two cheetahs lolloping from around the back of the house. I promptly closed the gate for fear of letting them out, although I wasn't too sure whether they were meant to be in there in the first place. More importantly I closed the gates out of fear of them getting too close to me. This was not what I had expected, most people have dogs guarding their house, not cheetahs.

Chris then came out of the front door. Luckily he had been expecting me, and shouted that it was okay to come in. I'll admit I was a little bit reserved in opening the gate, I was now only 2m away from two wild animals. It was all rather surreal. Both cheetahs quickly lost interest in me and walked away while I gingerly got my bags out of the car. This was going to be a memorable stay, I was sure of that!

Cheetahs are interesting animals. They are easily domesticated and historically were often kept as pets. However, once cheetahs are familiar with man, they lose their hunting and survival instincts and cannot be reintroduced back into the wild, unlike my friend the caracal.

These two cheetahs had been taken in when they were cubs and had therefore become used to living in a semi-domesticated state. They were fed carcasses on the back lawn, sharpened their claws on the garden trees, and wandered inside the house as if they owned it – which to my mind they probably did.

That night was Chris's birthday and we celebrated by having champagne outside under a wonderful, star-lit sky. The steak was on the braai and we were listening to the sounds of the wildlife. I was truly content at that moment. What more could a girl want?

Chris asked me about the projects I was running. I turned my head to answer him, whereupon I found myself being eyeballed by one of the cheetahs, which was only 20cm away from my nose. I opened my mouth slowly to answer his question, (sudden movements are not good in these circumstances), when the cheetah leaned forward and licked me on the arm. I know that cats have rough tongues, but this felt like I was being industrially sanded. I was genuinely surprised to find that my skin was still intact and not flayed to the bone.

What more could a girl want?

A cheetah's kiss will do nicely.

'The Face of Sibebe' Challenge

I scared myself stupid and agreed to climb Sibebe Rock with my friend Anna and what I didn't realise was that we were going to climb 'The Face of Sibebe'. Anna nonchalantly suggested we do it and I naïvely agreed, after all I do like a challenge. What I didn't realise was that I was going to push myself right to my limits, bordering on the panic zone but I try not to remember that part.

Sibebe Rock in Swaziland is a massive granite dome that looms over two valleys. It's the world's second largest monolith, after Australia's Uluru, and is the world's largest exposed granite pluton. It is 350m high and the gruelling route we were going to take was aptly named the 'steepest walk in the world'. Looking up the rock it is sheer, looks slippery and is obviously dangerous if you should fall. I had heard that Sibebe can be dangerous and that serious accidents have happened when people do not use their common sense. People start the climb and then cannot retrace their steps due to the extreme gradient, and then get into further difficulties.

Today we were not going to use our common sense. When Anna had initially suggested climbing Sibebe Rock I was delighted. It would be a great end to a fantastic trip to Swaziland and I had never been to the top of Sibebe – which is not a great thing to admit considering I represent Swaziland in the UK. I had tried several times but on each occasion had to come down after 100m because some of my guests were not that confident on the steep slopes. So, I was really pleased I had been given this opportunity.

I arrived at Anna's to make lunch before setting off and, while we were buttering our sandwiches, she suggested climbing 'The Face'. Anna's house is at the base of 3lbebe so I could peer out of a window and look up at the dauntingly high rock. I'll admit at that point it did look steep and I suspect that my eyes were out on stalks. Anna reassured me that it was possible and that people had done it before, in fact she had. We made an agreement to go to the base of 'The Face' ascent and make a judgement call from there.

It was a short drive and we were out of the car and getting ready to climb before my brain could compute the enormity of the task that we had set ourselves. There was no turning back.

As we started climbing everything seemed to be okay. Yes it was steep, but doable. The initial part of the climb was relatively easy. I could just about stand up, although I did have to lean towards the rock face, but it was manageable. I just had to keep going to keep up my momentum. Anna was ahead and was our route finder. There is no particular route up the rock face although every now and again you can see where some people may have trodden.

After ten minutes of upward climbing I was on my hands and sometimes my knees, there was no way of standing upright without a high chance of falling backwards and off the rock. It took all my concentration to find the best handholds and footholds and to ignore the screaming of my muscles as they overworked themselves. I had not done much exercise for the past six weeks and this climb was really taking its toll.

I felt happier following a route on the pink,

granite surface than on the darker granite. Mentally I'd convinced myself that the darker granite was slippery. This was probably not the case although I had had a couple of moments of scrabbling on the dark rock before I found a small ledge to prevent myself falling further back down the rock face.

We moved from one clump of grass to the next and at times I found myself kneeling on them to alleviate the pain in my legs. This was certainly turning out to be one hell of a challenge. There was a moment when I gently nudged my panic zone. I shouted to Anna to keep talking to me – I cannot remember what she said but I just needed something to concentrate on rather than what I was doing! The trick is to just keep going and keep that forward and upward movement, and to not think. Stopping is not a good idea, as I discovered later.

I don't think I have ever climbed up something so steep before without ropes or a harness – risk assessments aren't a major part of an outdoor-lover's activity schedule in Africa. I would certainly never consider taking anybody up the routes that we did but I have to say the exhilaration when we got to stop and look at the views was monumental. The only thing was, when we were near the top I thought that we had come out of the 'danger zone', but I have to admit I had a little wobble just before the top as my feet lost purchase and I couldn't make my legs work properly.

It took fifty-five minutes of upward purgatory we to reach the top. And wow, was the view rewarding.

When I looked down the face that we climbed up I was surprised that we had made it.

Anna also admitted that although she knew

people who had done it, it only numbered four!

She said that she had been wanting to climb it again for a while and a number of people had asked her not to do it, including her mum. She said she had confidence that I would say yes, that I would be up for a challenge, and that I would be stupid enough to do it. Well, what are friends for?

We ate our lunch overlooking an incredible view, while I had a fit of the nervous giggles fuelled by an overload of adrenaline.

There are lots of different ways to walk up Sibebe, in fact there is even a gentle track on the other side so it is accessible to all. However, we didn't see a single person on the way up (obviously!), but also at the top, and for most of the way down. Near the bottom we met a local man who was climbing up the rock to go to his homestead on the other side.

That night I dreamt that I was running away from something, scrambling around on all fours – my fingers hurt in the morning. I will certainly climb Sibebe again, it is highly recommended. If you hear me considering climbing 'The Face of Sibebe' again, you have my permission to shoot me.

Feeding Baby Rhinos

There was a snuffling, snorting, and mewing sound as the two baby rhinos anticipated their midnight feed. I was a bit blurry-eyed as I staggered downstairs to prepare their formula milk. I imagined it was like feeding human babies, except that the quantities are vast! We are talking litres here, not a little bottle.

I had been invited to stay at Mkhaya Game

Reserve in Swaziland and was roped into helping to feed a couple of baby white rhino - not the normal thing you get asked to do when someone offers you a bed for the night.

I arrived late afternoon, just in time to see the rhino have their 6pm feed. They were born in December 2015, just when a drought had really begun to impact on grazing animals. White rhino are huge grass-eaters and therefore need massive quantities of it each day. Unfortunately, due to a lack of grass in the game reserve, the female adults had not been able to eat enough to lactate. The result of this was that the young calves had to be removed from the care of their mothers so they could be hand-fed.

During the day, the rhino roamed freely in a large enclosure and spent their time in the company of a couple of Swazi ladies who expertly controlled the boisterous animals.

The first time I saw them I spent fifteen minutes hiding behind a tree, while the smallest rhino (a small one being over 200kg) cavorted on the other side. I knew well that I would certainly come off worst if contact was made. There were a number of large tractor tyres in the area so that suckers like myself could dive into them for safety. Rhino cannot jump very high at all, in fact less than the height of a tractor tyre, which was just as well as I used those tyres a lot.

In the evening the rhinos would come in for the night and stay in a room in the house, a room made rhino-proof with secure doors and matting on the floor.

These rhinos were being fed every three hours, around the clock, which was exhausting for everyone concerned – especially those doing the midnight and 3am feeds. This was where I came in. I was shown how to mix up the formula for each infant rhino (they were slightly different because one was male and the other was female and they differed in size). I was also given instructions on how to sterilise everything before and after feeding, and how to feed them safely.

The formula milk was made up in two-litre plastic drinks bottles with a teat on the end. While feeding, the two main concerns were to stop the rhino from guzzling the milk too quickly, and to prevent them from sucking the teat off the bottle and swallowing it. I was shown how to hold the bottle with my index and second finger wrapped around the teat so that I could alter the flow by pinching it and keep hold of it if it unexpectedly came off the bottle. The easiest way to do all of this was to shove your fingers, with teat, into the rhinos mouth... not for the faint-hearted!

There I was, at half-past midnight holding four plastic bottles containing milk and warm water and the sound of over-excited baby rhinos with the anticipation of being fed. As they are rather boisterous and exuberant during feeding there was a chest of drawers immediately inside the door. When you opened the door outwards you were face-to-face with the chest of drawers and not a charging rhino. I could then lean over the barrier and feed the rhino without having my shins fractured. They were demanding, probably because they were hungry, but once the teats were in their mouths they suddenly calmed down and it was easier to manage them. What a wonderful experience being that close to young rhinos, a real privilege to experience.

After a swift change in bottles, and ensuring both rhino finished their feeds at the same time, the youngsters settled down quickly. By the time I'd finished sterilising bottles and had got things ready for the feed at 3am, I could hear the gentle snoring of baby rhinos behind the door. Who knew that rhinos snored?

Piggy, Piggy, Piggy

"Piggy, Piggy, Piggy," called Margaret as she opened the door to go outside. This was followed by a tap-tap-tapping noise from one of the darkened corridors in the house and then into the daylight charged a bush pig hoglet. He was about the size of a bag of sugar, had pale, yellow stripes running horizontally along his brown barrel of a body, four tiny legs tipped with dainty hooves, big brown eyes, and a snout that never stopped snuffling. He was adorable to look at. He looked like an over-sized humbug.

Piggy, (yes that is his name – not very original I know but he didn't complain), had been found by Derek and Margaret as they were taking a late afternoon walk. He had been wandering alone in the bush. It was during the 1992 drought in Zimbabwe, a particularly harsh one, and Piggy had probably been left behind accidentally by his family after being separated from them due to lack of concentration or panic. Or maybe his mother had died of starvation, that was a common occurrence that year. We will never know why he was wandering alone in the bush, but he was far too small to survive by himself.

An adult bush pig is a strong, stocky creature with

powerful forequarters. Its upper tusks are barely visible, but the lower ones are razor sharp and can grow to 7cm in length. It is dangerous when surprised in the bush, or wounded during hunting, and it can inflict serious wounds with those protruding canines. An adult boar measures up to 90cm at the shoulder and can weigh as much 60kg. Formidable animals, not to be underestimated.

Apart from suckling them, the sows leave the care of hoglets to the dominant boar. Once hoglets are introduced to the group, boars assume the role of protector. Hoglets then remain in the group until the age of six months, and thereafter are evicted from the group by the dominant pair. Piggy was much younger than six months, more likely around two.

Derek and Margaret bundled Piggy up and had taken him back to their home in the bushveld. It was a desperate time and animals and people did extraordinary things. Here, he got acclimatised to this luxury and was probably living a right royal life in comparison to that of his long-lost pig family. He was fed leftovers and scraps from the food bins, slept inside, and had his own little bed in the corner of the living room.

Early on in his life with Derek and Margaret it was discovered that he loved having his tummy scratched. It was a most amusing thing to watch; you could scratch his tummy whilst he was standing up and he would make a loud grunting noise of pleasure, he would then go into a trance, and as his eyes closed he suddenly became very still. Then he would literally topple onto his side, legs stretched out and he would continue grunting for as long as you scratched his tummy, which could be ages as it was as much a pleasure for us as it was for him!

It's a strange sensation, scratching a bush pig's tummy. The hairs are thick and coarse whereas the skin is soft and supple. After a while the process would certainly wear your fingers down, but the amusement factor of scratching and listening to him grunt outweighed any potential damage to fingertips. He didn't like being touched anywhere else, which he let us know by use of a squeal and a sharp nip, although a gentle stroke along his flank was just about acceptable.

Piggy was a regular part of life in Zimbabwe and every time I visited Derek and Margaret, which was a lot as I lived next door, Piggy was always there vying for a tummy rub. He practically became part of the furniture and as he got bigger he became more noticeable – his presence in the vegetable garden being most obvious! He gradually grew in height and his humbug appearance diminished as his stripes faded to a reddish-brown colour, and he started to grow a bush pig's iconic dorsal crest of long, white hair. I often fell over him as I emerged from my house in the morning because he liked to sleep on the matting outside my front door.

One day, he went missing. It is amazing how attached you can become to an animal, even though you know that he's wild and should really be back with his own kind. We liked to think that he had found a sounder of bush pigs and joined them back in the wild. He was sorely missed by us all.

I missed him as I walked out of my front door, in case he was ready to trip me up, I missed giving him tummy rubs, and I missed watching Margaret get irate with him as he bulldozed her vegetable garden for the umpteenth time.

A year later, Margaret came running up to me, very excited, saying that she had seen Piggy. I couldn't believe it, how on earth could she recognise him?

"Come with me," she said, pulling me along, "and call him."

"Piggy, Piggy, Piggy," I called tentatively, thinking that Margaret was having a laugh at my expense, or maybe the sun had affected her. From around the house, trotted an enormous bush pig making its way toward me as if it was the most normal thing in the world to do.

I froze. To be honest I didn't know what to do, this pig stood about 70cm high, was muscle-bound, probably had good biting teeth, and could potentially inflict serious injury on me.

"See, it's Piggy," Margaret said excitedly.

"Really?" I replied sceptically.

"Go on, scratch his tummy... you'll see."

I looked at Margaret is if she was asking me to befriend a spitting cobra. I slowly approached the wild pig and tentatively held out my hand, fingers upwards in preparation to scratch his belly. What on earth was I thinking? He didn't move, so I closed the final gap between us until I could tickle his tummy. There was that familiar grunting noise, admittedly lower than I had been used to and certainly much louder. He fell into his familiar trance-like state and then toppled over, just as he'd done when he was a hoglet. Only this time the ground reverberated with his impact. I had to stifle a laugh.

The hairs on his tummy had grown thicker and I had to really scratch hard to get the right reaction. He loved it, and was happy for all of us to scratch simultaneously.

Adult Piggy had apparently crawled under the compound fence, leaving a family of pigs on the outside, and brazenly walked over to the house. His family didn't seem too happy with the situation. Piggy was oblivious to their concern as he was in a rapture of mammoth, tummy-rubbing, proportions. After a while we'd had enough and, as we stepped back, he righted himself, stood up, and stretched out his muscles. He promptly trotted over to the fence, crawled underneath it, and was reunited with his 'other' family. I was left with rather smelly hands, and sore fingers.

Piggy had simply come back to say hello and have a tummy rub, but his real family was now out in the bush.

NON-SENSE

Some stories defied classification by a single sense, but I simply couldn't leave them out. So, here they are, collected in a chapter called Non-sense. See what I did there?

Lightning Storm

After all the foggy days, the weather began to clear up. As we began the walk the sun was shining. I was with a couple of friends, Jason and Bryony, and we had planned an overnight walk in spectacular Drakensburg mountains in South Africa.

Our luck was in as I had been expecting a dull and dreary walk with the rain belting down. Judging from the people we saw who had just come down from the mountains this seemed to be the case. I have not been so in awe of scenery like I was with the Drakensburg, incredible, rolling hills, clear blue sky that highlighted the bright, golden colour of the slopes and the craggy tops piercing the heavens, located between South Africa and Lesotho.

We ambled up to the hut. It only took four hours at a dawdle, so we had plenty of time to relax and marvel at this creation.

The hut was a little blip out in the middle of nowhere. It was made of stone, with a thatch roof. I was expecting a floor to sleep on, and to have to fetch our drinking water from the nearby stream. Not a bit of it, there were beds, a table, sink, and even a flushing, yes flushing, loo. We were the only three people up in the mountains and had the hut all to ourselves.

After lunch we had planned to go exploring, but instead we did nothing but chill out and organise supper. We were planning to eat cold pasta, left over from the night before, but with the fire that Jason had got going we attempted to heat our meal up instead.

As we ate supper Jason said, "Wouldn't it be great if we had a massive thunderstorm during the night and bright blue skies in the morning?" We all laughed.

As we were sitting around the fire eating supper there was a sudden, gigantic crack, and a bolt of lightning erupted from directly overhead and divided into seven prongs which hung over us like a spider. Wow! I have never, ever, been in a thunderstorm quite like that one. We were actually in the middle of the storm although there was no rain.

I put down the dish that I was eating out of, there was no way that I wanted to be in contact with any metal that I thought might attract the lightning. I even took off my jewellery. I honestly thought I could feel them humming with electricity. My companions thought I was bonkers.

The three of us sat there, with our mouths open, gawping at the spectacle around us. It seemed as if it was our own private firework display. In the distance, there were bolts of electricity hitting the ground and flaring upwards on impact. I imagine they were hitting the huts in the community areas as they have metal over the apex of the thatching to prevent water from leaking inside. At this point it dawned on me that the roof of our hut also had metal along the top, for the same reason. The metal resembled a piece of screwed-up toffee paper and wasn't covering the top of the hut. This was not proving to be the best place to be in a storm.

The storm continued to rage and we watched silently. A slight shift of the winds redirected the storm back towards us and we unceremoniously chucked all our gear into the hut and put the fire out – the last thing we needed was a raging fire as well as lightning to contend with. We removed the mattresses from the metal beds and laid them on the floor in front of the door so we could still see the storm wreaking its wrath.

It approached us and we had to lock the door to keep it closed and to prevent the strong wind from lashing rain into our house. There was a wooden table in the room and we put our mattresses on the table and slept on them. It was a mite squashed to say the least, but anything was better than sleeping on the metal enforced floor. I was wary about going to the metal loo, being caught there would be an undignified way to go!

One bolt anywhere near the hut would result in the roof going up in flames and possibly us with it. Bryony and I were ready for this unlikely scenario and were wearing some of our outdoor clothes inside our sleeping bags, so that we would be ready to leap out of the burning hut. Jason found this highly amusing.

We said that we would not be sharing any of our clothes when we were all standing in the pouring rain watching the hut going up in flames with our belongings!

The storm continued to approach our tiny little hut and we watched its imminent arrival through the window. By now, the lightning bolts were so bright that they were hurting our eyes. At one point I accidentally looked directly at a bolt and I thought I had been blinded. Eventually, the other two went to sleep and I continued watching the electric sky feeling my heart go faster and faster. I was scared and, as the other two were asleep, I had to worry for all of us.

Just before dawn the storm abated and I got a few minutes' sleep before the sun came up over a bright blue morning – just as Jason had wished! Not a cloud in the sky. I wondered how the Drakensburg did not have clouds permanently sitting on the peaks. The colours from the sun bouncing off the slopes were continually changing with the topography and the walk back was just as good as the walk up the previous day.

My Patience and Public Transport

My patience and public transport will never go together. If there hadn't been a deadline for my journey I might have been semi-chilled-out. However, I didn't want to miss my boat transfer to Machangulo Lodge, and my escape to paradise.

I was travelling from Mlilwane, in Swaziland, to Maputo Marina. Ordinarily this was about a three-hour journey, but with prior knowledge of public transport and the lackadaisical approach everyone seems to have, I thought that I should double that estimate. That left me six hours to play with. I added an extra hour for the faff-factor such as border control mishaps, breakdowns, and the general laissez-faire attitude to timetables. I planned to leave Mlilwane at 8am. That left me 7½ hours as the boat transfer left Maputo Marina at 3.30 p.m. If everything went according to plan I should arrive in Maputo at around midday in time to order fresh calamari in the fish market and watch the boats arriving in the marina.

I ordered my taxi for 8am, was ready five minutes before, and waited. And waited, and waited. At 8.15am I called the taxi driver only to find out that he had cancelled my collection for some unfathomable reason. He apologised and said he was on his way. I eventually left Mlilwane at 9am, having used up my hour of faff before leaving. I wasn't worried, I still had six hours to get there.

Manzini bus station was an absolute nightmare – there were combis (small minibuses) crammed into every available space with drivers yelling their destination at the top of their voice. It was bedlam. I negotiated my way around reversing combis, groups of women with large buckets of water on their heads, and taxis hooting at feral dogs. I eventually found the Mozambique start point only to be told that a bus had just left. I was the fourth person on the next bus, it took twenty-two people... but it wouldn't leave until it was full. Brilliant.

The take-up for Mozambique was painfully slow, passengers dawdled in a steady flow and I began to get a nervous tic from looking questioningly at the woman in the little shack who was taking people's names and passports. Then, there was a flurry of activity with sign-ups... followed by an interminably long lull.

The bus arrived and it was not what I was expecting, I thought we would get a modern one, as this is what I had travelled on before, instead a piece of junk arrived that looked as if it had been patched together with sticky-back plastic and chewing gum. The whole 'vehicle' spluttered and battled and coughed and juddered. I imagined that we could all put our feet through floor and pick it up and run with it, Flintstone style.

We only had two more people to fill the bus and then we could go. It was 11am. At 11.15am an elderly gentleman arrived. At 11.30am I caved in, and bought the remaining seat so we could leave.

It took a further fifteen minutes to load the trailer, attach it to the back of the bus, and get everybody on board. We had lost half the passengers as they were buying meat, pawpaw, avocados, and potatoes in the neighbouring market.

Finally, the driver closed the doors and... he tried to start the bus and it failed. So, he opened the engine, fiddled with a few knobs, tugged a few leads, and it begrudgingly spluttered into action on the third attempt.

Going uphill out of the bus station would have been quicker walking. To prove that, a cyclist and a donkey-driven cart overtook us. It was noon, I was cutting it fine.

However, the bus made up for being so slow uphill by hurtling downhill at a death-defying speed that recovered some lost time. Maputo was at sea level so I thankfully calculated that there was more downhill than up. I estimated that we would make it on time.

I hadn't taken the border crossing into account. The Swaziland side was fine, we were all processed quickly and we walked into Mozambique leaving our dilapidated vehicle to get its transit visa. Mozambique immigration was a different kettle of fish. There was a rush on, as our bus was crossing one way and another bus was coming the other way. Two vehicles constituted a rush, with only one person to process visas, and he was on his lunch break. The frustration was getting too much for me.

At 2pm we were all on our way again after the rigmarole of pulling, pushing, tugging, and hitting parts of the engine to get it going. As we wound our way down the hill towards the sea I resigned myself to being late and not being able to dine on calamari. My main focus was making sure the boat didn't leave without me, so I made a few calls. I found out that the boat could wait for a little bit longer, but not too long because it was dependent on the tide. They were expecting me though.

I had some biscuits and crisps with me and I happily shared them with the passengers close to me. There were two older ladies opposite me who smiled in appreciation for the biscuits, three small children who were happy with lemon twirls, and a melee of adults who were all delighted with some food.

Only one person spoke English on the bus and he was sympathetic to my situation, having heard my frantic calls. "If it helps, I will have a taxi waiting for me at the bus station, you can share the taxi and we can go straight to the marina," he said. That's what it is like in Africa, there is always a plan to be made, people to help out, and someone to share experiences despite the laid-back attitude. I was enormously thankful.

At 3pm we arrived in a murky Maputo, chokka with vehicles. There was still time for me to catch the transfer.

My patience was tested again when my new-found friend's taxi driver was nowhere to be found. When he did materialise, ten minutes later, he didn't know where the Marina was. I sarcastically suggested by the sea as a good starting point. Showing the address, and with lots of gesticulating and explaining in English to siSwati to Mozambican and then to Portuguese, he eventually understood where I wanted to go.

The Marina was not what I was expecting and I wondered whether there was another one. It was a couple of rundown shacks, reminiscent of the bus station in Manzini, a few boats moored in a dank and dark enclosure, and not a soul in sight. I always imagined marinas to be large and wondered whether there was another one somewhere else. Was this really the right one? Was it the only one in Maputo? Surely not.

"You must be Jenny," exclaimed a man from one of the boats as he emerged into the daylight, "Ivor, from Machangulo Lodge. Great timing."

The relief across my face must have said it all. It had been a traumatic journey and my patience had been tested. I vowed never again, as I climbed onto the boat. Until next time, of course.

Over-friendly Traffic Cops

The traffic policeman, in an unusually bright jacket, stood in the road with his hand held up high, saluting the sky. I groaned inwardly as I knew I had been caught speeding. It is far too easy to exceed the speed limit in Swaziland, with its long, open stretches of road and a speed limit of only 60km/h (37mph). It is really, *really*, hard to stay on the right side of the law.

I pulled over to the side of the road along with the car behind me. We had both been caught. I resolutely got out of the car and went over to the cop and he directed me to his colleague on the speed camera.

"Here you are madam, speeding at 86km/h," he said as he pointed me out on the screen. "It is 60 km/h here."

I didn't really need to see myself speeding. It was just rubbing salt into the wound.

"Sorry," I mumbled.

"And here you are speeding sir, at 87km/h," he said to the gentleman behind me.

"You were both speeding."

We had the sense to look contrite.

"You were both going toooo fast," he said in typical laid-back Swazi style. A small smile crept onto his face as if he was admonishing school children. "Do not do it again. You need to pay a fine, see the lady in the car." By now, a grin was creeping across his face, not out of malice but out of sheer friendliness, with a hint of cheekiness mixed in.

I joined the queue for paying the fine to the lady cop in the car, there were quite a few of us. I was still not sure how this was all going to pan out. Everyone seemed so officious to begin with, but looked as if they were going to break into laughter at any moment.

"Licence please. Ehhaayy! What are you doing in Swaziland?" she asked, noticing my British license.

"I am a tourist, meeting a friend in Nhlangano."

"And tell me, how are you enjoying Swaziland?" She looked at me expectantly.

"I love Swaziland, it's beautiful. A great place to visit." I was glad that I could be honest about this statement.

"And how do you find the people," she asked as

she copied my name meticulously onto the speeding ticket.

"Really, really, friendly," I replied,

She beamed a smile at me. "And how do you find the Swazi traffic police?"

"Just as friendly as the whole of Swaziland," I replied honestly. This was true. She now had a massive smile on her face as she wrote out my fine for E60 (£3) in the appropriate box. Again, her smile was not because she was getting money out of me, it was the fact that I loved the Kingdom of Swaziland.

I handed over my E60 and received my speeding ticket, thanking my lucky stars that it would not mean any points on my UK licence.

"Hambanikahle," I said to all the police as I scurried to my car, it means 'stay well'.

"OOOhhh, Salekahle," they all chorused. "You know siSwati," they exclaimed.

We were all smiling now.

"Try not to go fast madam, eet is not gud."

As I drove away I could see the camera-man in my rearview mirror waving goodbye to me.

On my way back along the same stretch of road I made a conscious effort not to speed – well, at the points where I remembered where the cops were. Fortunately, they had all gone home anyway.

Swazi traffic police – probably the friendliest traffic cops in the world.

* * *

A few days later, it happened again!

"Driving licence," said the burly-looking police-man at the roadblock on the way to Simunye in Swaziland. He propped himself up on my car window as I rummaged through my bag to find it.

I handed over my UK driving licence.

"Is this you?" he asked pointing at the picture of me. I thought it was rather obvious that it was me, but I decided that it would not be a smart idea to state this.

"Yes, that is me, but it is not a great picture."

"And then this is your husband then?" he said, pointing to the smaller identical picture of me on my licence.

"No!" I said indignantly. "That is also a picture of me, they are the same."

"Oh, then this is not your husband then?" I shook my head.

There was a pause.

"So where is your husband?"

"I am not married."

Another pause.

"Then I can be your husband."

Lying to a police officer is never a good idea but I thought maybe a small one might ease the issue away from my marital status.

"I don't think my boyfriend would be very happy about that."

"Is your boyfriend in Simunye?"

"No, he is in the UK."

"Why is he in the UK when you are here?"

This was getting complicated, I could feel myself disappearing into a black hole.

"I am going back to the UK in three days' time." I said as I reached for my driving licence and closed finger and thumb over one edge, I was tantalisingly close to getting it back.

"Then I can be your husband for the next three days then," said the non-smiling police officer, still not relinquishing my licence. You have got to hand it to the guy for trying, I wasn't going to get away easily and there was a mini tug-of-war going on over my documents.

"So, the next three days then?"

"I don't think so."

"He won't know."

I leaned towards him slightly and gave a large, and what I thought, winning smile, whilst concentrating on gaining full possession of my licence. I won the contest and put it back in my bag.

However, the traffic cop was still propping up my window. We looked at each other. I smiled again and turned on the ignition.

"My name is Robert." He smiled, a beaming large one.

"Pleased to meet you Robert," I said as I engaged gear. "And Salekahle."

In my haste to leave I nearly collided with a passing car, then I would really have been in trouble.

As I'd said to the previous officer, Swaziland traffic cops are *very* friendly!

A FINAL THOUGHT

I hope that you have enjoyed this sensory journey through Africa. I've been incredibly fortunate to have had these experiences, partly as I took every opportunity that came my way, and partly because it was the job that I chose.

For me, Africa is restoration for my soul. I don't think I could survive a year without my regular 'fix' of Africa, and I'm not even considering trying.

I think everybody has a place where their senses come alive, it could be by the sea, in the mountains, Central America, or New York, but for me it is when I am in the southern African wilderness. There is something serene, something calming, something rejuvenating about living and breathing Africa.

ABOUT JENNY

I had no idea what I wanted to do in life. All I knew was that I wanted to do something that was connected to nature. I remember thumbing through the Edinburgh University prospectus, looking for courses as I really wanted to go there. The course on ecology sprung out at me. I thought it was for me. I did a bit of research, liked the idea, looked at other universities that did the same sort of course, and applied for it. It was a simple as that.

After that decision was made, my first disappointment was that the Ecology Department at Edinburgh University was miles away from the student union (and anything else for that matter), so I was upset about this. This led me to visiting Leeds University on a cold, snowy day, where I completely fell in love with the city and promptly put Leeds down as my first choice.

My school, on hearing this, was not overly enamoured about it and I remember one teacher saying, "Goodness Jennifer, are you really going to go up north and scrabble around in the dirt?" To which I succinctly replied, "Yes."

I loved Leeds, got a mediocre Honours Degree in Ecology, which I was pretty hacked off about as I thought I'd worked hard and at least deserved a better mark, and then started looking for a relevant job. I knew that I wanted to work in conservation, to travel, and to save the world.

Jobs in Saving The World are pretty hard to come by, and I spent 1½ years writing to every single conservation research centre based overseas, getting in touch with anybody I knew and contacting companies all over the world. I even wrote to Sir David Attenborough, and he wrote back wishing me luck in my job search, a personally hand written letter, which was incredibly inspiring. The fact that he had taken the time to write to me was extraordinary.

My mum was the instigator for my first job. She was talking to a friend on a golf course, whose daughter was a teacher at a school in Harare in Zimbabwe, who knew a lady called Pud who had two sons at the school, who was married to a guy called Jeremy Hill, who was a representative for Raleigh International in Zimbabwe. Raleigh International was looking for a permanent ecologist for a minimum of a year to help set up new conservation projects in Zimbabwe. How tenuous is that?

At the end of my telephone interview I was asked, "When can you get here?"

I replied "In three weeks."

Jeremy said "Okay, I'll have someone to meet you at the airport."

I hung up and that was that, I had my first ecological job overseas.

I was thrown into the deep end with concrete boots on. I'd never been to Africa before, I had limited knowledge about African savannah, and I had never met Jeremy Hill.

On arriving in Africa, I was given a clapped-out Land Rover that had no doors and no windscreen and needed to be push-started, a house with a resident Mozambique spitting cobra living under it, and a mud hut in the middle of nowhere. I revelled in it.

Although the contract was for one year, I stayed for two and I wanted to stay on longer. I had fallen in love with Zimbabwe. Forces were against me and, with the political situation changing rapidly, being a white, English woman didn't help. In fact, there was no way I was going to find another job there.

As fate would have it, I got a random phone call from a guy called Roy Hills, (no relation to Jeremy). He was looking for someone to work for the Vanuatu Protected Areas Initiative (VPAI). Roy had got my details from the Expedition Advisory Centre, where I had submitted my CV during my eighteen months of job hunting. VPAI were looking for an ecologist to provide scientific backup for management plans to help set up the first terrestrial (as opposed to marine) protected area in Vanuatu.

We had a long telephone call and he asked me whether I would be interested, I said yes, and he said we would be leaving in three months. I hung up the phone and promptly went to get an atlas. I had no idea where Vanuatu was.

The Republic of Vanuatu is an archipelago comprising around 100 islands located in the south-west Pacific. It used to be managed jointly by Britain and France until it gained independence in 1980. I was going to spend nine months living in the jungle doing scientific survey work.

I was given a blank canvas. Nobody had done any

scientific work there for a long time, so any data that came back would be helpful. I had support from Birdlife International and the British Sound Archives as both had large gaps in their information about birds in Vanuatu.

During those nine months, I: slept in a hammock; lived off the land; dug my own latrine; washed in half a bucket of water a day; spent months learning all the birdcalls; spent two months doing scientific data collection; got lost in the jungle for half a day; met a cannibal; led a funeral procession; and ate fruit bat. It was an incredible experience, so much so that I went back again for another nine months a few years later.

Out of those two visits, I wrote scientific papers, numerous reports for difference magazines and became the world expert in the Vanuatu Megapode – a bird that is a bit like a chicken that lays its eggs in the sand and gives no parental care to its offspring whatsoever. I've now lost that status. There are people who know much more than I do about these birds, but it was weird being asked if I would fly over to Sydney to speak at the world Megapode symposium. I didn't go, it would have cost too much, but the whole idea of it made me giggle.

Back in the UK, I continued with my scientific surveys and saving the world and worked for the Wildlife Conservation Research Unit based at Oxford University. Here I radio-tracked mink for analysis in removing this introduced species from the UK. They were having a major adverse impact on otter populations. I also radio-tracked badgers to provide information about badger perturbation due to bovine tuberculosis. The radio tracking of mink and badger was during the night, so I didn't see the light of day for three months.

I also analysed the innards of swans looking at the impact of lead weights and fishing tackle on them. That was rather smelly to say the least.

After my second stint in Vanuatu I realised that I wasn't cut out to be a pure scientist. I am rather gregarious and found the solitary scientific work lonely.

I've always been interested in mountaineering and hill-walking. This stems back to many a family holiday in Scotland to visit my grandparents, and my dad dragging us up numerous mountains. Unsurprisingly, I went through the process of doing my Mountain Leader Award and, having got this, doors opened up to me. I became a freelance expedition leader and led many charity treks to far-flung countries such as Vietnam, Costa Rica, Peru, and Morocco, as well as becoming a Duke of Edinburgh trainer for the expedition element of the syllabus. This meant I was managing to get more work in the UK.

Africa was calling. My heart was still there and I needed my fix. As I applied to different companies who I knew worked out there, one company called Quest Overseas was looking to branch out of South America and into Africa. Quest is a gap-year company and provides 12½-week expeditions for students. This is divided into 6 weeks of project work, whether it be community or conservation, and then 6½ weeks of expedition, where the group travels around experiencing different adventurous activities and teaches students to travel independently and safely.

Lucy King (who already worked for Quest) and I

took it upon ourselves to set up the whole Africa section of the company. We went out to Africa and did the 6½ week expedition route in two weeks, whilst simultaneously planning it. I then became the main expedition leader for the Africa section and helped train future leaders. We set up the project phases of both community and conservation in the Kingdom of Swaziland.

My first visit to Swaziland was in 1999, with Quest Overseas. I was back in Africa. I led back-to-back expeditions, which is thoroughly exhausting but brilliant. However, there was only so much time you can spend: a) making sure that drunken students don't wander off into the dark and into the path of a hippo; b) putting them into a safe airway position because they are inebriated; or c) listening to the inane conversation of teenagers.

Don't get me wrong I loved it, but after a few years it can get wearing and I wanted to do something for myself. I wanted to work with adults or school students and that was why Sense Africa, my company, was born. I set up Sense Africa so that I could get paid to go to Africa – that was my goal. It was a lifestyle choice and I wouldn't have it any other way.

Sense Africa has now become more than a regular fix for me. I love organising peoples' holidays and adventures and hope that guests leave Africa with the same love and admiration for this dark continent that I have. I hope they truly sense Africa for themselves.

Sense Africa has now become more than a regular fix for me, I have discovered my vocation in life. I love organising peoples' holidays and adventures and hope that guests leave Africa with the same love and admiration for this dark continent that I have. I often guide in Swaziland and love imparting the knowledge that I have picked up over the years as well as unusual facts and folk stories. And then of course I need to visit lodges and new areas to make sure that my knowledge is up to date, I know, it is a hard life. Yet, I cannot imagine doing anything else.

I hope everyone who visits this continent truly sense Africa for themselves.